Good Things Are Happening

Good Things
Are
Happening

RONALD ROOD

The Stephen Greene Press

BRATTLEBORO · VERMONT

The author wishes to thank the J. B. Lippincott Company of Philadelphia for allowing him to quote from *My Orphans of the Wild* by Rosemary K. Collett with Charlie Briggs. Copyright © 1974 by Rosemary K. Collett and Charlie Briggs. Reprinted by permission of J. B. Lippincott Company. The picture on page 165 is from *My Orphans of the Wild*, by Rosemary K. Collett, the J. B. Lippincott Co., publisher, and is used by courtesy of the J. B. Lippincott Co. Except as credited to others, pictures are by the author.

This book has been produced in the United States of America: designed by R. L. Dothard Associates, composed by American Book-Stratford Press, printed and bound by The Colonial Press. It is published by The Stephen Greene Press, Brattleboro, Vermont 05301

Library of Congress Cataloging in Publication Data
Rood, Ronald N
    Good things are happening.
    Includes index.
    Summary: A naturalist looks at what people
    are doing to save their part of the planet
    1. Conservation of natural resources—United
States—Citizen participation. 2. Conservation of
natural resources—Canada—Citizen participation.
I. Title.
S930.R64   333.7′2′0973   75–8194
ISBN 0–8289–0260–7

75 76 77 78 79 9 8 7 6 5 4 3 2 1

Contents

Finally, brethren, whatsoever things are true, whatsoever things are honest, whatsoever things are just, whatsoever things are pure, whatsoever things are lovely, whatsoever things are of good report; if there be any virtue, and if there be any praise, think on these things.

PHILIPPIANS 4:8

Good Things Are Happening

IT WAS TO BE QUITE A TRIP. My wife, Peg, and I had planned it for more than a year. We'd written some three hundred letters, made dozens of phone calls, pored over maps of the United States and Canada. Our library of field guides and travel books would have done justice to a Smithsonian expedition. From the looks of all the preparations, you'd have thought we were going to search for a clutch of dinosaur eggs.

And I guess we were doing just that, in a way. We were seeking evidence of something that seemed to be virtually extinct, from most reports we'd heard: any glimmer of hope that our weary planet would survive its struggle with people and their wasteful ways. If you can believe the news, we're trapped forever in a downward spiral, determined to pave, pollute and populate ourselves right off the face of the earth.

However, Peg and I weren't sure we'd heard the whole story. Wasn't there another side to the coin? In all this world of bad, wasn't there anything happening that was good? Wasn't there a person, here and there, who was having a positive impact on his or her surroundings?

And so we started out. We left Vermont in a January snowstorm. Driving south and west, then north and east, we covered 24,000 miles in our search. When we returned to our

1

own Green Mountains on a balmy morning in June, we had visited thirty-two states and four Canadian provinces.

But we had done more than take a glorified cross-country junket. We kept our eyes and ears open; we talked to more than five hundred people. And we found the answer to our question: There are plenty of people who are treating our soil, our waters, our wildlife with the love and respect they deserve.

One thing we can say for certain, now: you *bet* there's another side to the coin. And it's time people heard about it.

The men, women and children that Peg and I met on our journey across North America are a determined lot. They have been undismayed by the problems facing our outdoor world today. Hearing dire predictions that there is no hope for our forests and fields and wildlife, they've refused to believe them. Or, even if the reasons for gloom seem overwhelming, they haven't run scared.

Rather than size up a task as impossible ("Why, it'd take a government grant and a million acres to set aside those mountains for wildlife!") they have scaled it down to where they can tackle it themselves ("Let's see—what can I do to make that abandoned lot a better home for wayward raccoons?"). In so doing they have turned from the big, disheartening Negative to the smaller, more manageable Positive.

Don't get me wrong, however. The million-acre preserve is vital. What is saved today is all we'll ever save. But don't look for such great and worthy causes in these pages. You must go elsewhere if you want to climb aboard an airboat and ride the threatened Everglades with an anti-jetport group, or sit in on a court battle between Good Guys and Bad over the fate of a stand of giant redwoods.

No. There will be no great and worthy causes here. *Little* causes, yes—and often, just as worthy. Grassroots efforts that have been fruitful, somehow, without a government grant, a national campaign. It's true that here and there we'll snoop through the files of a county or state organization, and we'll even spy on one of the largest military bases on our continent. These, however, are the exceptions.

Most of the time we'll be "neighborin'," as my Vermont friends would say—walking the fenceline, for instance, with a teenage lad who singlehandedly transforms an abandoned oilfield into a nature preserve. We'll take a ride with the manager of a snack bar as he suddenly realizes that the streets look as if they've been sprinkled with oversized confetti—most of it from his eatery—and we'll see his novel solution to the problem. We'll become denizens of a floating forest, whatever that may be, and tramp the Ontario woods with a group of wolf-howlers, whoever *they* may be.

Consider it this way: imagine that a catastrophe has hit the countryside. The trees lie where they have fallen, and the ground is parched and bare. No birds sing, no insects buzz in the afternoon air. Nothing seems to be moving; the whole area has become a desert.

Look closer, however. Down at your feet is a brave little sprig of green. A seedling pokes up through the fallen ruins of the tangled tree trunks. A tuft of moss and a fleck of lichen gain a foothold and begin to make new soil. Trickling water gathers in a hollow and forms a little pool. Even in all this death there is life.

So it is, indeed, with our natural world. All around us we see the disheartening changes wrought by our passion for progress. We read about these changes, and see them on television; we contribute millions of dollars to heal the wounds and clean up the mess. Daily we are reminded of our compulsion to waste, uproot, exhaust.

Yet, if you only look, healing is taking place. So great is our concern at some new injustice done to our natural world, however—and so vocal may be the outcry—that the signs of this healing are forgotten. Rather, it seems there is no hope at all.

Well, 'tain't so. Not, at least, in the minds of the people you'll meet here. Two women in a New England town survey a line of stumps where giant elms once arched a boulevard before they fell victim to the dread Dutch Elm Disease. Placing a gaily-colored geranium on each stump to serve as a bright little stopgap, the women descend on the startled town fathers and wheedle them into replacing those rotting stumps with new and hardier species of trees. An Indiana man, faced with the prospect of a world gone bleak without the welcome song of the bluebird, creates a mini-refuge on his own half acre. Then he persuades his neighbor to do the same. They are rewarded by the first pair of nesting bluebirds in their town in nearly twenty years.

"Unfortunately," one of the heroes of this book told me, "we often stand with our mouths open while some expert tells us we're going to hell in a handbasket. Well, I'm not taking any unwanted ride just because some guy says so. Me, I'm dragging my feet!"

Thomas Carlyle put the same point another way a century ago. "When the oak-tree is felled," he said, "the whole forest echoes with it. But a hundred acorns are planted unnoticed by some passing breeze."

Like the fallen oak, most everything seems to have its compensations. I once had a teacher in school who never gave true-false tests. "You won't find many things in life that are entirely right or entirely wrong," she told us. "Why should we make the distinction here?"

One door closes; another one opens. Here in Vermont the state had an annual "Green Up Day" each spring after the snow had melted; thousands of volunteers cleaned the streams and roadsides of litter. The first year, U.S. Interstate Highway 91 was closed to traffic to dramatize the program. The governor flew over the state in a helicopter to check on the progress of the cleanup.

Like many such efforts, the campaign ran out of steam after a few years. Yet the idea continues in unofficial "Green Up Days" all over the state. Youth groups, garden clubs and sportsmen's organizations knew a good thing when they saw it, even if they had to go it alone, with no official blessing. Now, in April and May, you can still see carefully collected little piles of rubbish and plastic garbage bags along the roadsides, waiting for the pickup truck.

You can see similar sights elsewhere than in Vermont, of course. And that is the point: people working on their own. "We just felt like it," two New Brunswick teenagers told me when I asked why several of them were grooming and cleaning the edge of a highway on a July afternoon. "Besides, it looked as if the road could use a little help."

Here they are, then: a few score of plain people from Quebec to Florida, from the Maritime Provinces to the Hawaiian Islands who, considering some struggling plant or animal or bit of land, have realized it "could use a little help." Undaunted by Carlyle's fallen oak, they've gone ahead and planted the acorns—complete with a little elbow grease in the form of work and concern to help them grow.

I find their optimism refreshing in this world of doom and gloom. It is my hope that you will, too.

CHAPTER ONE

Voice in the Night

A THOUSAND PEOPLE stood in the dark, scarcely breathing. Men, women and children shivered—partly from the forest's chill, partly from a delicious tingle of fear—and strained to hear the voice in the night.

They were gathered around three rangers at Ontario's Algonquin Provincial Park. The rangers listened, too, but there was no sound except a twig that snapped under somebody's weight, and a muffled, nervous laugh.

The rangers waited another moment, then raised their voices for the second time, in a long, low howl. Somewhere, out in the nearly three thousand square miles of the park, was the object of their mournful call: that age-old master of the forest, the timber wolf.

There was no answer. The rangers tried a third time—and a fourth. Then, from a wooded hillside across the valley, came an answering cry. One wolf, unseen in the dark, lifted his muzzle in the ancient song of the wilderness. He was joined by another, farther off, in a primal duet that lasted perhaps five seconds—but stretched back a million years to a cave, a fire and shadowy forms beyond the circle of light.

The wolves fell silent. Somebody turned on a flashlight. A low murmur arose from the listeners. Car doors opened, headlights glared, and man became civilized once more.

"It wasn't much of a show, I suppose," a friend wrote to

6

me in describing the affair. "But I felt, when I had heard that howl, that I would never be the same again."

Those rangers, in coaxing a response from two of Algonquin Park's estimated three hundred wolves, had taken advantage of a peculiar habit of these wild cousins of the domestic dog. Like their civilized counterparts, wolves may add their voices to a raised, continuous sound. Why they howl is still not known exactly, but just as the neighborhood dogs will tune up when the noon whistle blows, wolves occasionally react to a noise of the right pitch and quality.

Oddly, the sound made by the rangers does not have to be a perfect wolf cry. Several years ago, when my publisher, Steve Greene, and I were on a visit to Isle Royale National Park in Lake Superior, we learned that the wolves of that forty-mile wilderness island have been known to join in with all manner of sounds. One time a trio of teenagers walked to a hillside a short distance from their camp, planning to meditate to the soft notes of a flute. No sooner had the flute begun, however, than a timber wolf added his voice—and cut short the meditation, right there.

At Algonquin, rangers at the "wolf-howl" try to imitate the sound of the animal as closely as possible. The effect, on the one night in three when the great beasts finally join in, is such that people do, indeed, feel as my friend did, that they'll never be the same again.

The performance is more than a bit of showmanship, however. Visitors are not just taken out, unprepared, to hear the wolves. The sound of *Canis lupus* is the climax of an evening spent in a lecture about the wolf, seeing pictures of him, and learning of his loyalty to his kind, his wisdom, and his courage in the face of great odds.

Although wolf-howling is now an official activity at Algonquin Park, it began as an effort by a few people concerned over the plight of this great, shy animal. The wolf's travels about the park in winter could be studied by following his tracks in the snow, but little was known of his summer habits. So elusive is the wolf that an entire pack can melt away into the forest, leaving little more than a wisp of hair and a swaying leaf. So tireless are wolves as runners that they can stir themselves at dusk, take to the trail, and be thirty miles away by dawn.

To keep tabs on this will-o'-the-wisp, a unique scheme was developed. Early in 1959, Dr. W. W. H. Gunn made tape recordings of the howls of captive wolves and coyotes at Algonquin Park. Armed with these recordings, two biologists, Douglas H. Pimlott and J. A. Shannon, rattled off by truck on the park's network of roads. Every so often they would stop and play back the recorded howls to a silent forest.

On August 5, 1959, Pimlott and Shannon got their first reply. Shortly before midnight, deep in the park's interior, a group of wolves lifted their voices in response to those of their captive brothers.

The wolf-howl program, then, began as a study method. Today the program continues as a means of public education. When we visited Algonquin in 1973 we were given a pamphlet on the technique of howling.

"One place," the pamphlet stated, "is as good as another. . . . Drive along the highway, stopping to howl every mile or two. Park cars well off the pavement. Don't slam doors or talk above a whisper. . . . When all is quiet, start howling."

With the public wolf-howls, held during August, and the do-it-yourself variety, it is hoped that visitors to the park may get to know and appreciate the wolf. An evening at the park's natural amphitheatre, and the evening's spine-tingling climax, are an attempt by a chastened human race at last to begin to understand this vanishing canine that it has spent most of recorded history hunting down.

Peg and I camped at Algonquin Park in early June, before the onset of the summer's program on the wolf. We tented at

A bluebird in Iowa takes advantage of the efforts of bluebird bene-factors, whose homemade nest boxes, tailored to the bluebird, are helping the species to recover lost range.

Two Rivers campsite and watched a black bear rummage through the trash barrel a few feet from our heads—until an unopened soda bottle fell with an explosion that sent him scurrying off into the woods. We viewed the imaginative displays at the Visitor's Center, and pushed a button before a lifesized photo of wolves to hear a recording of their howls.

Our contact with the wolves themselves, however, was limited to a few pawprints in the dust and one scat deposit at the edge of a clearing. Oh, yes, and a tree stump along the trail that had apparently been watered by a passing member of the clan—if the antics of a little dog belonging to some campers could be taken as any indication. The dog slowly circled the stump with intense interest. Then he solemnly added his own signature to this woodland bulletin board.

The door of man's approval remains closed to these magnificent predators. Nor would they enter man's world if they could—notwithstanding the grim tales of trappers chased to their cabins by a pack of the ravenous creatures. No unprovoked attack of wolves on human beings has ever been proved. Indeed, wolves retreat from man's presence whenever possible. But with a little understanding—and Algonquin Park's unique program whereby man joins them for a few minutes on their own terms, so to speak—there may yet remain a place where timber wolves can cling to their rightful inheritance.

No fearsome predators roam the woods of another park in Ohio, some four hundred miles to the south of Algonquin. The greatest primeval chase to be seen there might be a beagle after a rabbit. Nevertheless, Geauga County Park was one of our favorite stops along the entire trip.

I guess the park (actually *parks*, as there are four of them in the system) impressed us because of the easy, natural way the beleaguered woods and wildlife are being given a helping hand. With a minimum of tinkering, the rivers and swamps, woods and brushland are allowed to follow their natural patterns. Thus left alone, they have produced a surprising abundance of life. Surprising, especially, when the location of Geauga County is considered: less than an hour's drive from Akron and Cleveland.

At one point, the Cuyahoga River runs along the edge of fifty-acre River Park, in the Geauga system near Burton, Ohio. Launching their craft there, boaters and canoeists can travel outside the park for twenty-three miles of the Upper Cuyahoga—one of the finest stretches of canoeing water in northern Ohio. Much of this river still remains wild and unchanged.

Lack of development in this park system does not mean "hands off," however. There are carefully positioned picnic areas in two of the four parks, and more than seven miles of nature trails. There are early morning bird walks, movies, publications. At River Park, for instance, a little flyer is given to visitors. It details some of the past history of the area as motorists view it from a boundary road:

"As you drive along the north roadway, you are following the path of the interurban railway which once brought passengers as far east as Middlefield. The abutments of the rail-bridge still stand in the river, abandoned since 1925."

More history is recounted as the viewer notes the piles of earth along the river's edge: all that is left of a turn-of-the-century scheme to drain a swamp near the town of Burton. The hope was that the rich swamp soil would grow a fine crop of onions. However, downstream residents objected to the dredging of the stream. This precipitated the so-called "Onion War of 1900," one of the first conservation battles on record. After the smoke—or the river—had cleared, the "onioneers" (combined onion farmers and engineers) retired to seek their aromatic fortunes elsewhere.

The visitor is invited to canoe down the still-unspoiled Cuyahoga. Along the river he may see a deer, a fox, a mink. A lunker bass may splash him or a teal may rise on whistling wings—almost within the shadow of big city buildings.

River Park's information sheet ends with a word of caution. "Whatever you find to enjoy about the river," it says, "remember that it is easily destroyed. Please insure the pleasure of those who come after you by keeping your litter in your boat, and by treating the wild things with the same consideration that you would use if they were your own."

Those remarks are the words of Duane Ferris, Park Naturalist. Duane, a man of dry humor and a twinkling eye, is a thoroughly enjoyable companion. He doubles as a chemistry teacher on school days, but whenever possible he doffs the lab apron for outdoor clothes. His office, at Geauga's six-hundred-acre Big Creek Park near Chardon, is a trailer, set away from the traveled roads so you have a hard time finding it. "But if people really want me, they just head for the nearest swamp. There I am, like as not, up to here in the gunk, and having a helluva time."

Duane loves kids and has plenty of wildlife walks and other nature activities. He has also helped develop a unique facility in the park: The Ruth Kennan Trail.

"Here's how this trail came about," Duane told Peg and me as the three of us walked along its wide expanse. "We were trying to decide the best use we could make of the park, now that we had acquired it. We puttered around, looking here and there, hoping that our proposed changes would be best for the plants and animals—and the people who'd entrusted us with public money, too.

"While we were out near one of the little roads, we noticed this car that came every day. A man would sit in it all alone. He'd look at the woods for an hour, and then he'd drive away.

"One day we walked over to him, wondering just what this daily visit was all about. We discovered that he was all crippled up with arthritis. He couldn't move much, and had special gadgets so he could drive his car. He told us he loved the trees and liked to sit and look at them, even if he couldn't go out among them.

"Now that was a real heart-tugger. Right then we knew there was one thing we'd do with some of our funds: we'd make a trail so he *could* get out among the trees."

Duane and the park planners also considered other handicaps that denied people the joy of walking outdoors. Perhaps if the trail could be made easy enough, it would serve people with heart and breathing problems. Possibly it might be constructed for wheelchairs; perhaps even for people who were blind.

After much searching they discovered a flexible asphalt. Laid on a suitable bed, it wouldn't crack with the frost. They built the trail wide enough so wheelchairs could pass at any point. The trail is level, with plenty of benches at frequent intervals for those who get tired, or just want to sit and enjoy the trees with their ever-present birds.

There are many labeled plants along the Ruth Kennan Trail, some with signs in Braille, as well as places especially useful to the senses of hearing, touch and smell—a thick bed of moss to walk on, for instance. The trail goes close to several different trees so visitors may feel the bark. Fragrant flowers, aromatic ferns and pungent mosses add to the enjoyment of the walk, which winds along for eleven hundred feet and delivers the visitor back to his starting place.

The trail is a memorial to Ruth Kennan, a beloved teacher who labored tirelessly for the establishment of the Geauga County parks. When she died in 1970 her friends donated more than a thousand dollars in her memory. In the park publication *The Green Diamond*, Duane Ferris pays tribute to this energetic woman, whose efforts have meant so much:

"There are those who excuse their inactivity in the cause of conservation by complaining that their personal efforts will have little effect. The memory of Ruth R. Kennan remains as a contradiction to such negative thinking. The results of her efforts live on in the parks, and in the lives of numerous individuals."

A few months after our visit to Geauga, I had occasion to remember the Ruth Kennan trail. I was on a tour—almost a pilgrimage—to Hampden, Massachusetts, east of Springfield. Hampden was the home of that beloved teller of animal stories, Thornton W. Burgess. When I was a boy, my parents sometimes read me the latest adventures of Peter Rabbit, Jimmy Skunk or Shadow the Weasel, as Burgess told them in the daily *Hartford Courant*. When I got up my courage to write to the great man, he answered with a kindly letter—so kindly, in fact, that I determined right then, at the age of seven, to become a naturalist one day.

Now, decades later, I stood at the entrance to the Laughing Brook Nature Center, on ground where Thornton Burgess must have strolled as he considered what story he would tell next. Ahead of me was the Laughing Brook itself, and upstream twinkled the Smiling Pool. Down in the woods I could tell where Laughing Brook joined Burgess's "Big River," the Scantic.

Something else had been added—and I am sure Thornton Burgess would have welcomed the addition. There was a bright yellow rope, about an inch in diameter and strung above the ground at waist height. Its undulating length followed a path that extended from the Center's parking lot toward the junction of brook and river. The rope was the guideline for a nature trail for the visually handicapped.

Signs in large print as well as in Braille were placed along the rope at intervals. A few feet before each sign, or before a marked change in trail direction, a wooden dowel was inserted in the rope to alert the traveler to new features just ahead.

At some points the sighted person was invited to close his eyes and experience the sounds, the smells, the feel of rough bark and supple branch, for himself. Closing my own eyes, I could almost hear the scream of Sammy Jay, the scolding of Chatterer the Red Squirrel, and the murmur of the Big River, where Mrs. Quack's husband had hidden under the bank and nursed his gunshot wounds.

Following this special path along the river, through the woods, and back to the parking lot, I realized that here was imagination at work. Refusing to be turned away by the barrier imposed by impaired vision, creative members of the Massachusetts Audubon Society, the State Federation of Women's Clubs, and other friends of Thornton Burgess have gone to the senses of smell, hearing and touch to help make the late author's home a welcome place for all.

An assistant at the Center expressed his thoughts after I had exclaimed about the trails, the roomy outdoor cages for wildlife, the many fine displays at the Visitor's Center. "Mr. Burgess liked birds and animals," he said, simply, "but he liked people, too."

We visited a number of areas for the handicapped over the United States and Canada. Increasingly, you find ingenious accommodations for the disabled in national, state and Provincial parks, plus almost uncounted local areas. We listened in on hearing aids at a small park in South Carolina where the songs of birds and the whispers of leaves are amplified, and chatted with a wheelchair fisherman at a special dock on the shores of Lake Champlain.

These areas, and others of which you may be aware yourself, are a recent and welcome addition to the continent-wide complex of parks, forests and refuges. The handicaps that their special adaptations help people overcome are handicaps in vision, hearing, physical strength—and, in every case, the more disabling handicap of imperfect understanding.

CHAPTER TWO

Bent Twig

"ACTUALLY," said George Schauer, "it's only a matter of degree. Working with gifted children is just like working with other kids. You've just got to work faster. The tree still grows as the twig is bent. At least that's what you hope."

Peg and I were standing with George at the edge of a woodland near Cochranton Public School, Pennsylvania. George teaches a class of nine gifted fifth and sixth graders in a special program at the school, and we were about to walk their brand-new nature trail.

The trail had been made possible when twenty acres adjacent to the school became available for educational purposes. The students consulted Owen D. Winters, naturalist at nearby Clear Creek State Park, about how to lay out the pathways. George Schauer assumed responsibility for seeing that the trail was completed.

As it turned out, "responsibility" wasn't quite the word. The students took the task upon themselves. All George did was watch them go. With the enthusiasm of kids everywhere, those youngsters pitched in with everything they had.

"They were after me at every turn," George told us. "If it was a good sunny day they'd try to wheedle me into taking them out on the trail. After school it was more of the same. And guess where we were on weekends."

George, however, did not really mind. He finds his students a lively challenge. "My real trouble," he said, "was not keeping after them—it was keeping up with them."

Together they did the job well. Starting with a tractor trail the Vo-Ag students had roughed out part way, that handful of irrepressible youngsters advanced through the forest like a stream of army ants, devouring—mentally—everything in their path. They studied nearly every inch of the proposed route, detouring to go past an interesting oak stump here, an aromatic sassafras bush there. A chipmunk hole received treatment worthy of a lion's den, and the trail was angled so it approached an abandoned crow's nest as if that derelict platform of twigs had been the top of Mt. Everest.

That was not all, however. There was more than just snooping into every hole and hollow tree. With the thrill of discovery came the wish to share discoveries with others. The students took photographs, asked questions and read books about items along the trail. Then they wrote out descriptive passages that would go in a brochure for the visitor to take with him as he walked the path.

This is where Peg and I came in. George Schauer invited us to go for a Saturday morning hike along the trail with two of his students, fifth graders Paula Vickers and Kathy Girardat. Our little group started up through an overgrown field, but soon Paula ran ahead. When we got to where she had stopped, we noted that she was standing beside a piece of cloth tied to a bush.

Then, almost as if we had pushed a button, Paula gave us a couple of paragraphs of "message" that, George assured us, was word-for-word with the as yet unprinted brochure.

Now it was Kathy's turn. Running ahead to the next wisp of rag on a bush, she gave us the whole story there, also letter-perfect. And so we traveled the mile-long trail, enlightened and entertained by a deadpan little oracle at every turn.

We finished our walk, and thanked our host and hostesses.

As we left them we realized we had been privileged to know two of nine potential "trees"—to use the bent-twig metaphor—already inclined by a talented teacher toward a deep feeling for the outdoors. And their efforts have borne more fruit, as well: a recent letter from George Schauer tells us that art, geography, science and photography students also use the twenty-acre nature reserve in the lucky town of Cochranton.

The trail was opened to the public, complete with lettered signposts, directional arrows and a little guidebook, a couple of months after our visit. And how did John Kerr, Cochranton Elementary School principal, officially open the trail? By cutting a ribbon with a pair of scissors?

Hardly. Not at this fun-while-you-learn project. Kerr and George Schauer had their ribbon-cutting ceremonies with a native vine and a pruning saw!

We visited a number of school nature centers all across the country. Many of them, like the one in Cochranton, have been acquired by look-ahead town fathers. Others are the gift of generous individuals who have shared with the community their good fortune in owning land. In nearly every case the whole town seems to benefit. Studies in agriculture, soils, water, conservation, forestry and meteorology go ahead while the birdwatchers, botanists, rock hounds and just plain outdoors people pursue their own interests.

In one half-acre yard of a tiny school in Raleigh, North Carolina we saw a science class studiously practicing the ancient art of dowsing, or finding underground water with a forked stick. In another reserve area, in Georgia, we watched in surprise as half a dozen students solemnly planted as many pots containing poison ivy. It seems there weren't any of the rascally plants for miles, and the class decided a little poison ivy along the trail would be an educational asset—properly labeled, of course.

Looking back over the many outdoor study areas we

Near Omaha, Lynn Myers interviews a great horned owl, a star member of the assembly of birds, mammals, reptiles and plants that make up the resources of an innovative program in school nature education.

visited, it's hard to tell which is best. I guess we're in the position of the mother who cannot say which child she loves most: each one is best. Certainly, however, Karlin Grunau and her students at Golden View School of Huntington Beach, California, are high on our own list.

We found Karlin at the back edge of the school property, arranging a number of wild food-plant specimens on a big piece of cardboard. She was surrounded by a dozen students. All of them were so absorbed in their task that we wandered about and took half a dozen pictures before anyone noticed us. Then the students merely made room so we could join the charmed circle, too—an unspoken tribute to the skill of a fine teacher.

When Mrs. Grunau disengaged herself from that group of rapt students, she started us on a tour of this Student Environmental Learning Facility—or SELF. She had another class waiting for her, but she introduced us to Scott Groves, a student who took time from his other classes to give us a tour of the school's fascinating two acres.

That special plot of ground started out simply enough, we learned: a chunk of wasteland next to the school. Overgrown and eroded, it was like abandoned land almost anywhere. Stones and weeds alternated with gullies and sandbanks. A fallen tree, almost hidden by brush, slowly rotted back into the soil. A swampy area half the size of a tennis court sent mosquitoes and gnats and other delights out daily to enliven the countryside.

Mrs. Barbara Dolf, principal at Golden View School, saw behind the disarray, however. More correctly, perhaps, she saw *into* it. Here was a chance to help the students follow the fortunes of a piece of land that was going its own way with little interference from man. Laid out into smaller plots, such as a wildflower area, woods and marshland, it might make a good place to learn about the outdoors right on the school grounds.

Mrs. Dolf secured the expert services of William Gaffaney, the school district environmental consultant, in laying out the facility. She has also had valuable help from Dennis Vogt, outdoor learning specialist. Thanks in part to Karlin Grunau's background of ten years as a ranger-naturalist, SELF became a fascinating little outdoor world for those enthralled Golden View students.

"Now we have a geology area, a native-plants area and a wildlife-food area," Karlin told us. "The old swamp is still there—it's one of our most valuable study areas, with its rich variety of life—and a little stream flows from it. We have left a portion of the grounds in the original state, too. The students can see it all—from those old gullies and brush all the way to our intensive-use area where we keep the animals."

The animals consisted of the school pony—curried and pampered within an inch of its life by those city-bred students—and various native mammals, amphibians and reptiles in season. Through the chance to handle and feed them—and occasionally get nipped, into the bargain—the students have gained a deep respect for living creatures. "In fact," Karlin said, "one class has been trying to figure how they could keep a coyote pup. Not that they have such an animal; they're just looking ahead."

This, we realized, betokened a new era in a land that traditionally greeted the coyote with the epithet of "varmint." Here were several dozen youngsters willing to give the hated animal a new lease on life. Through meeting animals and plants on a natural footing, they have learned that there are few living things that are all bad—or all good, for that matter. In the case of the coyote, they had decided, if man was foolish enough to pasture his sheep and other animals right in the coyote's front yard, man had to accept part of the blame for every lost lamb.

So the Golden View Student Environmental Learning Facility's initials, S–E–L–F, can be seen to be more than a convenient acronym. Students are, indeed, on their own as they look up the uses for a new plant they have discovered, or decide what animal made the hole under the roots of the thorn bush. Through trial and error they learn what food, shelter and nesting materials are best. "Occasionally we lose an animal we're caring for," admitted Mike Clark, one of the students, "but Mrs. Grunau usually helps in time if we're going wrong."

Karlin agreed that once in a while a child did, indeed, "go wrong." But she feels that the tremendous educational value of personal contact with well-loved—if sometimes mis-handled—plants and animals far outweighs the rare little tragedies that do occur.

Helping students to learn by doing is just one of the activities at SELF. Karlin Grunau is also a superb artist. She assists her pupils in developing their powers of observation by encouraging native drawing ability. Some of the drawings go into SELF's own newsletter. Peg and I received an impressive and authoritative document informing us that we had been elected to its official subscription list. This was a singular honor, as we were aware of the effort put forth by those students with every issue.

Karlin has one other talent—and this is a rare one, indeed. She has the gumption to quit while she's winning. As I write these words, a letter is open before me telling us that Karlin has taken a position with another school. "Its outdoor facility is limited at present," she writes, "but we'll see what we can make of it."

Peg and I know what she will make of it: another SELF, doubtless. This knowledgeable artist-teacher is about to give a few dozen more students a gentle nudge in the new but infinitely old direction of learning how to get along with the plants and animals around them.

The resources at the Golden View School in California are,

admittedly, limited, even though the rest of the school district's two dozen schools use them, too. Take the idea of
SELF, however, and magnify it nearly a thousandfold. Set up
its acreage in somewhat the same ways: untouched areas,
nature trails, swamps and creeks, pens for orphaned and injured animals. Add a nature-center complex of classrooms,
laboratories, libraries and an auditorium. Multiply the fine
teaching and interpretive staff, too, and you have the superb
facility known as Fontenelle Forest Nature Center.

Located a mile southeast of Omaha in Bellevue, Nebraska,
Fontenelle Forest embraces 1320 acres of gigantic trees, old
fields, Missouri River bottom and ponds.

The area is named after Logan Fontenelle, last chief of the
Omaha Tribe, who is buried there on his native land. Chartered by the State of Nebraska in 1913, the infant Fontenelle
Forest Association raised money to buy the first 364 acres.
Gifts of land from Dr. Harold Gifford, Sr. and his heirs, plus
a hundred-acre tract from Sara Joslyn, brought the total to
nearly nine hundred acres.

Other gifts and legacies—some tiny, some large—have en-
larged Fontenelle Forest Nature Center to a nearly three-mile
tract on a wooded bluff overlooking the Missouri River. Still
nonprofit and entirely privately supported, Fontenelle now
includes every natural habitat of the Cornhusker State, from
prairie to marsh to virgin timber. The historic past of the area
is well preserved, too, instead of being buried under tons of
concrete. There are the remains of Indian earth lodges five
centuries old, for instance. A part of the trail of Mormon
pioneers runs through the forest, and there's a site believed to
be an 1823 Missouri River fur-trading post.

Soon the fifteen-hundred-acre Gifford Peninsula, abutting
Fontenelle Forest, will be put into use. Then, in the words of
Virgil "Jim" Haggart, Jr., the Nature Center's president, the
Fontenelle-Gifford complex will be potentially "the finest
facility of its kind in the United States."

Peg and I were the guests of Mrs. Ruth Green, one of Fontenelle's part-time instructors. Blond, vivacious Ruth is a real farmer's daughter who married a traveling salesman—her husband, Bob, sells real estate. Ruth is popular with the small fry and their parents who arrive by school buses, chartered buses and automobiles—more than twenty thousand of the young visitors each year. She took us behind the scenes and introduced us to the birds and animals that were making temporary homes in some of Fontenelle's spacious outdoor cages. But when she took us out into the fields a few miles away, we also discovered what a good naturalist she is.

It seems that Ruth is a specialist in the art of identifying birds by their call notes. A faint chirp in the treetops would set Peg and me to craning our necks, binoculars at the ready, though Ruth had easily pinpointed the bird, and, like as not, was already listening to another. "Nashville warbler," she'd announce nonchalantly, while we were still hoping for that first glimpse.

At another point we slogged along through the mud at the edge of a swamp. On that May morning the air throbbed with the gurgle of blackbirds, the whistle of meadowlarks, the chatter of sparrows, the babble of shore birds. There was such a racket that it was hard to pick out any individual song. Hard for us, at least, but Ruth held up her hand. Then, motioning us to follow, she led us to a clump of cattails.

When a small brown bird fluttered up and away to a more distant part of the swamp, she nodded in satisfaction. "Aha!" she exulted, "I *thought* I heard a marsh wren!"

Ruth is the soul of patience with a group of kids. In our case, she gave us credit for knowing the songs of birds perfectly already, and felt that our ears were tuned to catch the subtle differences in their tones just as hers were—a flattering, but disconcerting, assumption. With beginners, however, Ruth will take an entire fifth-grade class, say, and carefully guide the students through a morning of sights and sounds.

She reduces the confusion of bird song to words and phrases.
"Hear that?" she'll ask, as students obediently cock an ear in
the proper direction, "the bird that says 'teacher, *teacher,
TEACHER.*' That's the trademark of the ovenbird. This bird
builds a nest in a leaf-lined cup in the ground. Somebody
thought the nest looked like an oven, and that's how the bird
got its name."

On she goes all morning ("the Canada Goose says *ekonk.*
There's an Ekonk hill in Connecticut that's named after the
sound of geese flying overhead"), giving an entranced group
of kids and their teacher a whole new dimension to the outdoors. Or, if one of those Missouri Valley storms is brewing,
Ruth keeps them closer to the main buildings. There the
youngsters meet the hawk who lost his wing to a careless
hunter ("Boy, I'd never shoot a hawk as nice as *that*, Mrs.
Green") or the rabbit whose eye was put out by an air rifle
("Wow! And I thought a BB gun was a toy!").

As Ruth points out, "There are thousands of people who
could share their love of the outdoors with youngsters like
these. They don't need any Fontenelle Forest to get them
started. All they need to do is try on their own. After all, the
ideal class is one student and one teacher."

Those classrooms and auditorium at Fontenelle are constantly busy. We looked at the large wall calendar that lists
the activities for the month: many days had four or five
events scheduled. Norm Kopecky had just finished a lecture
on frogs when we arrived; he was busy setting the stage for a
talk on the tall grasses of the magnificent prairie that once
covered the area. And those grasses are impressive too: Norm
is more than six feet tall, and the samples of big bluestem,
giant wild rye and Indian grass in his demonstration were
higher than his head.

Not every part of the region can take advantage of Fontenelle's resources, even though some students ride a whole day

on the bus to get there. However, fifteen miles west of Omaha, we found the next best thing to Fontenelle in an ingenious program that could be adapted to any part of the United States or Canada. When the schools can not visit the outdoors, the outdoors can come to the schools—if you work it right.

This traveling terrain is housed in a rambling building in a field in Gretna, Nebraska. Known as the Omaha Suburban Area Council of Schools Science Center—OSACS for short— it contains hundreds of living things. They are kept in well-maintained pens, tanks, terrariums and portable greenhouses.

Any teacher in the seventy-three member schools of OSACS can "check out" an aquarium, a turtle, a potted plant—or any of hundreds of other items—for a week or a month. Along with the plant or animal there are clear, detailed instructions for its care. There is a collection of assorted gadgetry, too, for the use of chemistry, physics and general science classes. A van-type station wagon makes regular rounds, picking up and discharging its living passengers and paraphernalia twice a week.

Mrs. Michael Myers showed us through the OSACS main building. "A fourth-grade teacher in Platteview can order a clutch of eggs," Lynn told us, "and an incubator to hatch them. Some weeks we go through ten dozen eggs. Or if any of our other eighteen hundred teachers is studying reptiles native to Nebraska, we'll ship him the greatest load of snakes and turtles you ever saw."

By sharing with each other in this way, schools can all benefit. Books, equipment and specimens get maximum exposure among some forty thousand students in the OSACS district. The Center's personable boa constrictor, aptly named Julius Squeezer, was originally housed at the Ralston High School, for instance. When he took up residence at OSACS he became one of the most popular denizens of the "living library."

Other interesting items among the hundreds offered include kits containing complete animal skeletons—dismantled—for use as a sort of classroom jigsaw puzzle. There's a physics unit on bouncing balls, plus a straight-faced instruction sheet on how to raise a bumper crop of mosquitoes. You can check out a recording of songs of the humpbacked whale, too—a sound rather rare in Nebraska.

Film loops available through OSACS include many fascinating subjects, among which we discovered a sedate demonstration of the art of burning candles, plus another with the intriguing title "Smear and Squash Techniques." (This latter, by the way, instructs students in the making of microscope slides.) Member schools can also sign out microscopes if they're interested—tweezers and test tubes, too.

"As far as I know, this is the only center of its kind in America," said Dr. J. Bruce Holmquist, the director of OSACS. "We are funded through the Nebraska Department of Education. However, what we are doing could be accomplished by any two or three schools working together on limited budgets. In this way they'd save unnecessary and costly duplication of resources."

There are other ways to beat the cost of materials and the headaches of maintaining your own little menagerie. Set up a school assembly put on by an outside speaker, for instance. Then even the dullest student may "catch fire" under the spell of a new face, a new voice, a unique idea. I remember hearing a talk on owls at school when I was a boy. The name of the lecturer escapes me, but the sight of his half-dozen owls, all solemnly zeroing in on me with those great eyes, left me intrigued with owls for life.

Similar exciting experiences of learning are in store today for the many students who meet my Vermont neighbor, Russell Marsceill, and his bees. Russ is a member of the local chapter of the Retired Senior Volunteer Program. RSVP, as it is

called, is a nationwide project that uses the talents of senior
citizens in ways that match their special skills. Two of Russ's
talents are a liking for people—especially children—and a
fondness for that industrious creature, the honeybee.

Russ lost a leg in 1970 in a traffic accident. With the loss
went his job as maintenance man at a local industry. "But I
decided to make the best of it," Russ said, "even if I did retire
five years early."

One of the pleasant tasks of RSVP is to make its members
available for talks at schools. "When calls came into our local
chapter in Bristol," Russ told me, "I realized that here was
where I might be helpful. To a lot of kids, every wasp and
hornet is a 'bee.' They never realize the importance of all
these 'bees' to our forests and meadows. Lots of wasps and
hornets feed on harmful insects by the hundreds. Honeybees
fertilize wild cherries just as they do cultivated cherries. They
make honey out of tree blossoms, as well as from meadow
flowers."

Russ often takes a glass-walled observation hive along on
his talks. He points out the queen bee, surrounded by her
attendants. He explains how the bees' seemingly random
activity is really organized into a pattern as precise as those
geometric cells of the honeycomb. Sometimes he captures one
or two bees from a hive in the area and places them in a "bee
box" baited with honey. When the bees have fed to capacity,
he lets them fly out a nearby open window. Then, to the
astonishment of the children, the bees return in a few minutes—with several other bees, who help them harvest this unexpected bonanza-in-a-box.

Russ Marsceill, like so many rural Vermonters, got most of
his education in the sunlit fields of the countryside he loves.
"But I've talked at colleges just the same way I've spoken at
kindergartens," he grins. "I've given repeat performances at a
school for the blind. There are so many things to tell about
bees that you don't really need to see them at all. And no

matter where I talk, some kid usually comes up afterward and tells me he'll never swat another bee as long as he lives."

On they go, the people who are busy bending those pliant "twigs," the willing pupils who will develop an ever-widening interest in the outdoors. Thousands of the twig-benders are hardworking school teachers, struggling to maintain a little terrarium, raise a caterpillar, or rehabilitate a field mouse orphaned by the cat of some tearful student. I remember such a teacher: Joseph Jablonowski, the biologist at our Terryville High School in Connecticut. His class was so fascinating that only years later did I realize that his low-budget laboratory contained only one microscope.

Even today, when I have some question about Connecticut wildlife, I'm apt to turn to Joe Jay, as he is now called. I often wonder how many other twigs he shaped in his long years as a teacher.

The thousands of other adults who are influencing youngsters to love and care for their surroundings include 4-H leaders, scoutmasters and youth directors of many kinds. There is the scoutmaster who guided his troop to clean and plant a strip-mined area in West Virginia, for instance, and the 4-H leader in Iron Mountain, Michigan who introduced us to his eleven youthful "beautification experts" along a roadside—nine of whom were in one family.

There is also King Baker, Outdoor Education Consultant in Hampton, Ontario. King shows Canadian teachers how to use live animals in the schoolroom. He backs his knowledge up with a printed pamphlet, "Creatures in the Classroom." He feels that students relate best to "concrete learning experiences, rather than abstract. A child handling a live animal learns care and responsibility first hand."

Another novel instance of outdoor education is the husband-wife team of Carolyn and Don Cruikshank, of the Institute of Human Understanding, Inc., in Rochester, Vermont. In sessions that may range from an hour's assembly to a full day, they take school children back to the time of the American Indian. They show the students how to sandpaint, work with natural materials, and learn of their wild neighbors in the outdoors.

Carolyn and Don gained their knowledge of Indian ways by close association with an impressive number of tribes. They have traveled and studied on many tribal lands. Peg and I have been guests at their summer High Rise Camp in Rochester, where the trappings of artificial life fall away—literally and figuratively. There a few dozen fortunate children learn the joy and beauty of living with respect for the land and its creatures. They learn to accept Rusty the fox, Goliath the fawn, Scratchy the porcupine—all wild, but ready to accept them, too.

There are outdoor education centers scattered all over our continent. They range from the tiny back-door wildflower patch that my friend the late Mrs. Henrietta Field, used to keep at her home in Ferrisburg, Vermont, to the eighteen-mile automobile nature trail at Joshua Tree National Monument in California. One of the greatest such areas is the result of the efforts of a man whose name most of us hardly know.

That man, J. Sterling Morton, knew his "twigs"—human and botanical—as well as any person of his time. He has been responsible for the growth of millions of trees in founding the annual observance known as Arbor Day.

We visited the peaceful grounds of the Morton estate, forty miles south of Omaha in Nebraska City. On the estate, Arbor Lodge's three-story mansion with its white columns is surrounded by labeled trees, shrubbery and plants of all kinds. Morton, whose son built the salt company that bears the family name, set out many of these trees when he and his bride moved to Nebraska in the 1850's. He felt so strongly about the lasting value of trees as living monuments that he persuaded Nebraska Governor Robert W. Furnas to set aside a day in April for tree-planting. First designated in 1874, Arbor Day was officially fixed by the Nebraska legislature in 1885 on April 22, Morton's birthday. Today most states and many towns have established their own observances of Arbor Day.

Thousands of trees are planted each spring in Arbor Day ceremonies. Millions of children watch as Class Trees are solemnly set out in campus soil. Some of these children may be impressed for the rest of their lives by the beauty and permanence of trees.

More trees are planted to commemorate great events, anniversaries, visits of important people. Peg and I saw a line of these living monuments along a road in Hilo, Hawaii— planted by, or on behalf of, presidents and their wives, movie stars, world figures of many kinds.

As J. Sterling Morton, who became U.S. Secretary of Agriculture, said in an Arbor Day address in 1894: "Other holidays repose upon the past—Arbor Day proposes for the future."

Looking to the future, too, is a woman half a continent away from Morton's Arbor Lodge: Wendy Holmes, on the banks of the Hudson River. She is concerned with the fate of the river, and of the plants, animals and people who depend on it.

Each great river has a distinct personality. When the Nile is mentioned, you're apt to think of a fertile delta, papyrus, ancient pyramids. A few women wash their clothes at the water's edge, perhaps, while keeping a watchful eye out for those crocodiles. The Mississippi conjures a picture of gracious hospitality, cotton bales, possibly an old stern-wheeler.

The Hudson, however, has no such tranquil associations. To many of us *Hudson* means *pollution.*

In large measure we're right. The Hudson is raw sewage— hundreds of tons of it dumped into the river daily from Manhattan alone. The Hudson is junk, from refrigerators, half

buried in the muck, to the recent newspaper photo of a floating cello set adrift by some melancholy musician. The Hudson is oil slicks, rotting ropes, foul piers—but seldom, if ever,
is it beauty, intrigue, romance. Cleopatra floated down the
Nile on a barge, and that was great. But on the Hudson?
Never.

The river is different to Wendy Holmes. She has lived next
to it for a quarter century. During those years it has taken on
more dimensions for her than you could see in a quick look.
Through hundreds of photographs, Miss Holmes has captured many of the moods of her gigantic neighbor.

Her photos show the seamy side, yes; plenty of it. They
show a young couple strolling blissfully among the bedsprings
and bottles. They show police scuba divers probing through
floating crates and old tires for the body of a suicide. But her
pictures also show sparkling waves; glittering lights reflected
in a mirror-like surface; the wistful faces of the homefolks as
they watch the departure of an ocean liner. Her photos show
fish, too, and eels, and fishermen—for tons of striped bass and
herring and shad are taken annually from this supposedly lifeless stream.

With support in part from the New York State Council on
the Arts, Miss Holmes poked around abandoned piers, beneath the George Washington Bridge, onto the decks of tug-
boats, exploring the river she loves.

"I remember explaining to a policeman that I was working
on a book on the Hudson River," she says in introducing a
portfolio of her photographs, "and he nudged his buddy. 'Did
you hear that? She's writing a dirty book!' "

Wendy Holmes knows well the pollution of the Hudson.
"We have ruthlessly fouled the river, it is true," she admits.
"But I have found that the story does not end there. I have
tried to show the rest of the story in this portfolio revealing
relationships between the tugmen and fishermen, the Coast
Guard, the Stevedores, policemen, businessmen, captains,

tourists, scientists, and others who share a community in New York's waters."

And show the story she does—sometimes tenderly, sometimes bluntly—but always with compassion. Nearly fifty of Wendy's dramatic prints are gathered in the collection titled *Hudson City—The Living River*. They are published under the aegis of a unique organization, the Wave Hill Center for Environmental Studies, in the Bronx. Right within the confines of New York City, the twenty-eight acres of Wave Hill command a fine view of the river and the New Jersey Palisades. There, among the gardens and brushlands and greenhouses, visitors from kindergarten age to adult regain a lifegiving touch with the wild world—a touch they may have thought was lost forever in the great city they know as home.

Like Wendy's pictures, the many-faceted Wave Hill program covers every angle. There's a Geology Trail, for instance; self-guiding so the observer may go along at his own speed. It starts him right where he stands: in front of the marble steps of one of the buildings. Probably every city dweller has seen marble or felt it or walked on it. The trail guide points out that the marble was once soft limestone, laid down in a prehistoric sea and transformed by heat and pressure into the hard rock of the steps.

At another stop the guide invites the reader to examine limestone for himself. With a hand lens he can pick out the fossilized shells of the organisms that swarmed in those ancient waters.

The trail takes the traveler to where he can gaze across the Hudson to the Jersey Palisades—another familiar sight to many New Yorkers. There, as he reads about them, he can almost feel the ground shake beneath the great dinosaurs that roamed this area when those columnar cliffs were formed. And, still keeping the visitor where he is, the guide invites him to feel and examine a familiar object, indeed: a brick in a nearby wall. Here, he discovers, he is in the presence of one of man's earliest building materials—baked clay. On he goes, noting the sandstone of the "brownstone" housefronts of New York, plus outcroppings of the bedrock on which the city's skyscrapers stand. And so on, to the end of the walk.

At Wave Hill, the Nature Trail and the Wild Foods Trail meet the urban explorer, too. He discovers that the tree on the corner of his block is a veteran city dweller. He finds its name to be *Ailanthus*, the Tree of Heaven, whose peculiar virtue lies in its capacity to absorb all the polluted air man's devices can belch its way—and lift its leaves for more. He learns that the common plants in his neighborhood's vacant lots are more than just anonymous weeds. They are known as Lamb's quarters, the optimistic herb that pokes up in nearly every bit of exposed soil—and tastes like good, fresh spinach.

There's much more to Wave Hill than nature trails and greenhouses, however. There are wild areas, woodlands, rocks. There are field trips for school youngsters. A training program helps visiting teachers to make use of the facilities on the grounds of their own schools. There are films, lectures, bird walks, plant sales, and a flood of publications crammed full of information on everything from agriculture to zoology.

Florence Cassedy Gallagher, Administrative Assistant at Wave Hill, has the contagious enthusiasm that seems to pervade all those twenty-eight acres. When I asked her for information, she deluged me with nearly ten pounds of notes, clippings, and photographs. She gave me a list of the competent staff and its distinguished guest lecturers. She even presented me with a facsimile invitation to attend the 1972 ceremonies that had established Wave Hill as a National Environmental Education Landmark under the United States Department of the Interior. It is one of only eleven sites so named in all the United States. Fontenelle Forest, Nebraska, similarly honored the year before, is another.

Writing to her "alumnae association," Cass Gallagher tells

the story of this surprising little gem of natural history within the confines of New York City. Since the gift of the Wave Hill estate to the City in 1960 by the Perkins and Freeman families, approximately ten thousand school visitors a year—plus the general public—have come to find new meaning in vacant lots, overgrown roadsides and their own backyards. Cass cautions against overoptimism, however. It cannot be easy for a child to relate a cool forest glade to his crowded city block. "A former Hudson River estate," she says, "is hardly the background against which many persons are silhouetted every day."

Richard Madigan, Wave Hill's director, has stressed education since the center opened in 1968. Under his guidance, the aim is to help students and adults realize that we live as a part of the outdoors, rather than away from it.

And there's always the Hudson. A special program studies it almost constantly and invites others to do so, too. Although Wave Hill is frequently in the news, one staff member, Joe Tobin, a few years ago acquired more than the usual recognition. In August, 1970, Joe and several dozen young people drifted slowly down the lower Hudson in canoes in a "funeral column" to dramatize the slow decline and death of the river. Above each canoe trailed a helium-filled black balloon: a funeral for the air as well. The procession was held during the morning rush hour, to gain maximum exposure to motorists along the traffic-clogged West Side Highway. It was viewed by thousands more on TV that evening.

And did the funeral procession accomplish its purpose? It may be too early to say, although interest in the fate of the Hudson is livelier than ever. Certainly the sight of those canoes with their silent black balloons will be hard to forget. And, as one of the canoeists pointed out, "We didn't do anything great, perhaps. But neither did we just sit around and gripe. At least we did *something*."

Doubtless some who saw the procession had seen Wendy

Holmes's photographs, too. Her camera and those canoes: ordinary objects put to an extraordinary use. Perhaps even now the gears are turning somewhere, finally to mesh together—and the "dirty book" will get results.

Wendy Holmes and her talented camera have recorded the delight and wonder of children at Wave Hill as they learn how raindrops make rivers and valleys. She has photographed the fascination of their elders as they watch the youngsters. She has seen them both so deeply absorbed that the real problem is to turn them off when it's time to quit. And, as a Wave Hill staff member, she has smiled as children have recoiled in shock to the suggestion that Henry Hudson, on his voyage of 1609, must have tasted the water of the lower river to find out if it was fresh or salt.

"After all," said one child, "it was polluted, wasn't it?"

CHAPTER THREE

Little Candles

THE GEORGIA SUNSHINE filtered down through the new-budding trees as we arrived at the little house. A white-haired woman hurried out to welcome the four of us. "Great of you to come!" she said.

Our friends, Fred and Peggy Spencer, had introduced us to Florence Lynn over the phone. Now, with the Spencers, we were guests of this remarkable woman. In speech and manner like the birds that had become her life, Florence was bright and cheerful. "Come on inside," she urged. "We don't have long to wait."

She guided us past bird feeders, nest boxes and food platforms to the door. Once inside, we took a minute to become accustomed to the dim interior. We were in a darkened part of Florence's kitchen, with the only illumination coming through a canopied and tree-shaded window in its front wall.

It was dark in there, yes, but not dismal. The darkness gave an air of anticipation, as if we had entered a theater where the show was about to start. Florence was the usher who showed us to our front-row seats. And that is how I felt as we perched on the kitchen stools and looked out into the yard: like an audience at a theater. All it needed was the overture.

The birds, of course, supplied their own music. They chirped and called as our perky hostess took a seat beside us. "I love to hear them," Florence said, "and watch them. But I also want others to enjoy them. That's why I have this end of the kitchen darkened—so my guests can come and go, and even fidget without being seen. In fact, I've even had people go to sleep on me."

There'd be little danger we'd relax that much, however. We had looked forward to this visit, and had arrived right on schedule: half an hour before the anticipated appearance of one of the southeast's threatened birds. Known as the red-cockaded woodpecker because of an almost hidden patch on the sides of the head, the bird has been on the decline for years. Now we were about to see this rare species for ourselves.

"Birds are creatures of habit, just like people," Florence told us. "They run on a timetable. One bird feeds at a certain time; another arrives later. Jays are apt to keep banker's hours, while some of the sparrows are here before dawn. The woodpecker should be along after it has finished at my neighbor's feeder."

While we waited for the woodpecker, we watched as scores—sometimes hundreds—of birds settled down in Florence's yard. Although there were a number of food platforms scattered about, the entire yard was really one continuous feeder. Seeds and husks covered the ground like gray, crackly snow. We saw a dozen cardinals at once. There were mockingbirds and redwings, plus a few robins. Over and around them was a constant flurry of smaller birds, almost like the drifting leaves of autumn. They were busy processing one mouthful after another of birdseed, peanut hearts and assorted fruit through those little innards.

"They eat more than ten pounds of food a day," Florence said. "That's two tons a year. Lucky I can get the peanut hearts from a processing plant, or they'd eat me into the poorhouse. Most of the birds just love peanut hearts."

We gazed, enthralled, at the fantasia of color and motion just beyond the window. We enjoyed another treat, too: the privilege of witnessing an expert teacher in action. Florence called out the names of the new arrivals, giving little hints to help recognize them:

"There—by the pine—three cardinals and a white-throat. Notice their strong beaks for crushing seeds? Here come the bobwhites; looks like ten of them today. The males are nattier than the females—that's because they don't do any work. And, see? Over on the old picnic table, the myrtle warblers? I always spot them by those little yellow feather patches. . . ."

Spurred by her enthusiasm, we compiled a list of nearly two dozen species in as many minutes. Some, like a pair of brown-headed nuthatches, were year-round residents. Others, such as the robins and a hermit thrush, had dropped in from their northward migration on this late February day. "Yesterday a hawk swooped in and panicked 'em all," Florence said. "You never saw such a commotion—but wait! Here comes what we're looking for!"

We followed her gaze to the lower limbs of an oak. A black-and-white bird, a bit smaller than a robin, clapped up against the bark at the end of a long glide. We could see the zebra stripes crossing its back, the distinctive white cheek patch. It flew in so easily and began to peck at a chunk of fat so nonchalantly that we found it hard to believe it wasn't as common as pigeons in a park. Yet here in Fortson, Georgia, as all through its southeastern range, the red-cockaded woodpecker is scarce indeed, the victim of an odd quirk of fate.

Like most other woodpeckers, the red-cockaded is a valuable helper in destroying forest insects. It nests in a tree whose interior is hollow or dying, a household preference it shares with many other woodpecker species.

The nesting tree of this bird is a pine—and only a pine affected with red-heart disease. Here the woodpecker's needs run counter to the wishes of man. Red-heart, as its name implies, destroys the center of the tree. It is an infectious disease, so a single blighted tree represents a threat to its neighbors.

Quite understandably, foresters have tried to eliminate red-heart from their holdings—and thus have all but eliminated the home of their valuable woodland ally.

For years the struggle of the red-cockaded woodpecker went unnoticed. People felt it was just getting less common, and that was all there was to it. Then, when man realized that if he cut all the red-heart trees he'd wipe out a good feathered insect trap, he had some second thoughts. Thus, today, in the few areas where pine and red-heart and the red-cockaded woodpecker still exist together, a belated truce has been declared in the war of disease eradication.

"People still need the most cash per acre of trees," Florence Lynn admitted. "However, the forester is now aware of the problem. Some lumber companies mark a 'den tree'—where a red-cockaded has its nest—with a special paint. Then, woe to any cutter who downs one of those trees. He's got to talk fast to explain a paint spot on one of his logs."

Florence's concern goes beyond the birds that come to the feeders in her yard, however. She tells her friends to keep watch on any of the woodpeckers that they see: where they come from and where they go. Then, by careful tracking, a party of searchers can home in on a den tree. Finding the owner of the land, they impress on him the value of that tree and its feathered residents. "If you can't locate the landowner, or if he looks as if he wants to call the little men in white coats, you just quietly find the nest, say nothing—and hope," she admitted. "Most of the time the owner is happy to see that the tree gets protection."

After the woodpecker we were watching in Florence's yard had eaten its fill, it flew away as suddenly as it had come. Knowing that it might be headed for its nest, the five of us piled into the car and drove in the direction it had taken. We parked on a sandy knoll, walked fifty feet—and there, in the side of a pine, was the woodpecker's home.

We gazed at the three-inch entrance hole twenty feet

A little blue heron forages in a lagoon near Sanibel, Florida, where encroaching development has increased awareness of the value of a healthy outdoors populated by wildlife.

above our heads. Like most den trees of this bird it had a characteristic "threshold area" devoid of bark for several inches around the opening. There was little about it to mark it as the final retreat of a threatened species.

The woodpecker apparently had other visits to make, however, or perhaps he had flown again before we arrived. After waiting for some time for one last glimpse, we returned to Florence's home. There we bade her a reluctant goodbye.

As we drove away, Peggy Spencer put the past two hours into words: "Florence Lynn teaches without trying," she said. "Hundreds of people have 'taken the course' in that kitchen. We've brought her a number of friends, ourselves. As for the woodpecker, she takes what steps she can to save it. She gets people interested and concerned. She doesn't just stand there and wring her hands."

As I considered those words I realized that Peggy Spencer, too, had done more than "just stand there." By taking people to meet Florence Lynn, from whom they learn of the woodpecker's story, Peggy has done her part in helping these embattled birds. Indeed, without people like Fred and Peggy Spencer all over the country we'd have been just another writer and his wife on a research trip. As it was, friend passed us along to friend in a sort of transcontinental handshake. I was reminded of three kids I once saw who were sharing a single ice cream cone, lick by lick. Unlike the cone, however, we gained instead of losing in the process.

The Spencers were like Bob and Mary McCullough, for example. Bob is a biology teacher; we had found his name in an outdoor publication and had telephoned on a hunch. Learning of our search for man's favorable impact on his natural world, the McCulloughs invited us to pay a visit. "We've got friends you can call on all over the country," Bob said. "We're starting a list for you now."

On the strength of his invitation, we scheduled a stopover

at the McCulloughs' home in Burton, Ohio. They did, indeed, have a multitude of friends. Through them we met a game warden in Texas and a wildlife researcher in Denver. The McCulloughs gave us the address of Don and Martha Linton, neighbors of theirs who wintered in Sanibel, Florida, and who opened their home to these two strangers from Vermont.

And they introduced us to Gladys Mills.

Miss Mills lives on fifteen acres, a few miles from the Mc-Culloughs, in the northeastern Ohio town of Chardon. Her house, reflecting the long years of work that have been her way of life, is unprepossessing and without frills. The crinkles around her eyes and her forthright manner of speech tell of long hours in the open, with trees and animals for neighbors.

As we settled down to a cup of tea, Gladys told her story.

"Well," she said, "it started several years ago. I chanced to see two small boys playing across the road from my driveway. I said to myself, 'two boys playing tag: fine. Whacking at things with a baseball bat: also fine. But throwing stones at everything in sight? Not so fine.' "

"When they started throwing things," she continued, "I knew it'd be only a matter of time before they hit something—maybe one of my birds or a squirrel. So I decided to step right in the middle of it. You know me—that's the way I do things."

We hadn't known Gladys, of course, but we were learning fast. Here was a woman who'd speak her own mind, even to a couple of the neighbor's kids six and eight years of age. But how do you reprimand two boys whose only fault is that they are full of the dickens?

This was no problem for Gladys, however. "I just called them over to my yard. 'Do you know where your baseball bat came from?' I asked them."

The boys told her it came from the store. "Then I asked where the store got it, and they didn't know. So I pointed to that ash tree by the side of the path and said, 'It came from a tree like that one there.'"

She indicated other trees to the boys. One tree was responsible for their hockey sticks. Another supplied the wood for the picnic table. A twig from one of the young trees would make a dandy whistle. And would they like to see the plant that helped give the flavor to root beer?

They certainly would. So Gladys told them to return the following Saturday.

The next week they were back with two of their chums. They had a great time together on the paths through Gladys's property, learning to recognize common plants and animals.

At the end of the walk, they asked if they could bring some other boys next time. Gladys told them she'd welcome all their friends.

To make the walks more meaningful, Gladys improved on her woodland pathways. She cut away a branch here, a dead bush there, so as to show a wildflower or the den of an animal. She ended up with a nature trail more than a mile long, winding and twisting through those modest fifteen acres.

Now the walks became a bi-weekly affair. Every other Saturday a handful of children would arrive at Gladys's door, wondering what surprises she had in store.

Then a couple of parents appeared. Gladys welcomed them, perhaps with secret relief; a dozen exuberant kids sometimes can be hard to hold in check on a day when—to them at least—there's no school. The painless education process snowballed until more children, more parents, and even some grandparents brought the total of visitors to nearly three dozen.

"I've never studied a great deal," Gladys Mills admitted. "I got most of my education"—with a wave of her hand toward the window—"out there. And I keep on learning. I find something new every time, just as I did with those first kids three years ago."

It's not all an idyllic life for Gladys, however. She has been in the forefront of several fights where the woods and fields around Chardon have been threatened. "People see the chance to make a dollar on a chunk of land," she said, "and something snaps inside 'em. They just don't give in to reason, either. But I'm worse than they are. If I go to a meeting and there's something I don't like, I don't just sit there. I speak up!"

Long into the evening we listened to the adventures of this warmhearted, outspoken woman. Later, as we went over our notes with the McCulloughs, Bob said, "You know, Gladys Mills has done more with her fifteen acres than many a park commissioner with a six-figure budget."

Indeed she had. She was having fun doing it, too—as much fun as we were having in searching for her counterparts in thirty-two states and Canada.

The following day, as we prepared to leave, Bob gave us a roster of names and addresses three pages long. It listed some thirty people "who are doing what you're looking for, Ron: lighting their own little candles in the dark. They'll all be good for a story—and a cup of coffee, besides."

We scarcely felt the need for coffee at that moment, after Mary's hearty breakfast of pancakes and Buckeye maple syrup—which, even to a Vermonter, was delicious. But we were glad of the thirty names. Although I had written over three hundred letters in the past year in an effort to get the most out of our projected 24,000-mile trip, the recommendation of one friend to another can be more effective than a dozen letters that ended "Cordially yours."

As we looked over the McCulloughs' list, we saw that each name on it was, indeed, like a candle in the dark. There was Griffing Bancroft, for instance, whom I remembered from his days as a sportscaster on CBS radio. Griffing now lives in Sanibel, Florida, pursuing a lifelong interest in wildlife while firing others with his enthusiasm. Peg and I were privileged to attend one of his "twenty-mile talks," as he calls them: an all-morning ride with other guests in his station wagon.

As we drove along, Griffing pointed out a raccoon that sozzled with sensitive paws through the molluscan delights of a mudflat—plus the alligator that kept the raccoon from swimming across to an island where a number of ducks nested. He showed us a rookery of egrets that erupted like an exploding snowdrift as thousands of the dazzling white birds flew from the trees to their feeding grounds. He called the flowers and bushes by name and took us to one of the finest portions of Sanibel's fabulous shell beaches. Gifted with knowledge and ability, Griffing Bancroft shares his talents with visitors, opening their eyes, and so lighting more candles from his own.

Bob and Mary McCullough's list of names also told us of Malcolm "Mac" Kirk, whose efforts did much to preserve thousands of native orchids on Ontario's Bruce Peninsula, in Lake Huron. Although we didn't have the chance to meet Mr. Kirk, we were privileged to visit the land he had helped to save: the peninsula's incredible natural wildflower gardens at Dorcas Bay.

We walked beneath the Bay's pines and maples, feeling almost as if we should be on tiptoe. At our feet were patches of yellow ladyslipper, pink pogonia, dwarf purple iris, with an occasional shiny-green bearberry or red-veined pitcher plant in the boggy areas. A wood pewee sounded its lazy whistle from the branches of a pine. A great crested flycatcher flew out into an opening, snapped an insect, and drifted back to its nest, into which the inevitable snakeskin was woven. Ring-billed gulls called from the nearby shore. Were it not for the Malcolm Kirks and those who share their concern, Dorcas Bay and hundreds of places like it would be lost forever.

Then there is Cora Stencil of Green Bay, Wisconsin, who

teaches applied natural history to 4-H campers ("every kid gets in the mud, if I have anything to say about it"). Cora and her husband, Mike, had not only worked out an address list for us, but had arranged a potluck supper for Peg and me when we arrived in Green Bay, though we were only strangers they had met in the mail. Thus we could talk with two dozen of Green Bay's outdoors-minded people over the goulash and pie.

Candles, all of them: some large, some small. Cora Stencil's many activities have earned her the title of "Green Bay's most valuable natural resource." There are some five hundred others—from a modern Johnny Appleseed, south of Montreal, who tosses grain and other edibles where they might sprout for wildlife, to Florence Lynn, who began this chapter with her annual two tons of birdseed.

I wish I could mention all five hundred of them. Space, of course, does not permit. Nor would such a complete listing be prudent in all cases: my Johnny Appleseed friend's favorite toss-away, for instance, happens to be the small, seedlike fruit of the staghorn sumac. This scraggly shrub grows in almost any soil—from sterile sand to rich loam—and produces a berry-like cluster that's sought by everything from mice to mockingbirds. And it's a caution what my friend does with those fruit when he gets the chance.

He has been known to saunter out across some well-groomed golf course with a pocketful of sumac seeds, for instance. There, gifted more with a love of birds than of birdies, he thoughtfully sprinkles a handful of seeds in the sand trap.

CHAPTER FOUR

In Sheep's Clothing

HE'S A BLUFF, HEARTY MAN. You like him at once. Give that curly graying hair and beard a few more years to whiten up, and he'll not even need a suit. John Harris is a Santa Claus out of uniform.

No gentle reindeer accompany him, however. Far from it. His traveling companions are full-blooded timber wolves—by tradition the most dreadful enemies the reindeer have ever had. The mournful howls of the wolf deepen the chill of the moon-washed tundra snow. Their cruel jaws drip with gore as they pounce on their struggling victims, man or beast. Or so the legend goes. Small wonder Santa's reindeer took to the sky!

John Harris, however, scoffs at most of the stories. And he ought to know: his animal compound near San Francisco houses the largest private study collection of native wolves in North America. " 'Biggest enemy of the reindeer?' " he repeats, in answer to your question about the wolf. "I should say not. In many ways the wolf is the greatest friend the reindeer ever had."

This view, a turnabout in our understanding of the relationship of hunter to hunted, has long been a part of John's thinking, and indeed his very life. He seeks constantly to bring the whole picture of carnivores into true focus. Freed of emotionalism, tall tales and downright lies, the predatory

48

animal emerges as a creature quite different from the direful menace that we often visualize. John has taken it upon himself to help other people realize the importance—indeed, the necessity—of the carnivore in a healthy outdoors inhabited by wildlife.

This is where the wolf as a friend of the reindeer comes into the picture. The reindeer—and its close cousin, the caribou—travel in herds over the tundra, nibbling at vegetation along the way. Under normal circumstances the wandering herds will often be attended by a few wolves. A healthy caribou has little to fear; it can readily outrun a wolf.

Such "escorts" of a half dozen or so wolves may keep several hundred caribou keen, alert and watchful—qualities essential in the lives of wild animals. Let a caribou become injured or yield to advancing old age, however, and it begins to lag behind the herd. Possibly it develops a communicable disease, or it may have been born with an infirmity that could be passed to its offspring. Thus the disabled caribou actually poses a threat to its neighbors. The wolves quickly discover its misfortune, and soon put an end to its troubles. The entire caribou population benefits from this natural, normal process.

The wolves, of course, do not take the misfits because of any desire to improve the species. Cripples are just easier to catch. As John Harris points out, the good farmer keeps his farm thrifty and productive by culling and weeding. "A poor cow will eat almost as much as a good one," John says, "and a spindly plant occupies garden space needed by a healthy one. The wolf—or the weasel or the wildcat, for that matter—is sort of a wild 'farmer,' improving the 'herd,' whether it's rabbits or pheasants or deer."

Spurred by this conviction, John has turned a hobby interest in wolves into a campaign that has taken him to more than thirty states and Canada. With him travel one or more of his two dozen charges. John and two of his most famous wolves, Clem and Jethro, have visited more than three thousand schools and service clubs across the country. They have been featured on national television, and have been guests at Congress and the White House.

Excited youngsters have watched the great, friendly cousins of the domestic dog as they were brought on stage and more than three million eager hands have stretched out and petted them. On my first meeting with Clem, those powerful jaws closed around the hand that writes these words. The wolf gave the hand the gentlest squeeze in greeting—and released me with an amiable lick of a warm tongue.

John Harris and his wolves are not merely a razzle-dazzle show, however. "The most difficult part of the whole performance," John confided to me over coffee after an appearance at Castleton State College, Vermont, "is getting up there on stage. I know it's got to be done, but I keep hoping someone else can do it."

There are usually several "someone elses" to help John feed and care for the personable passengers in the rear of their van-type station wagon. Pamela Innes, who does publicity and admits to being "all cracked up" as she says, about their eighty-pound fellow travelers, accompanies them when she can. Sometimes she brings her two children, Albert and Timmy. Judy Bull, a researcher, and Aleta Pahl, a splendid artist, were along for the visit to Castleton, as was Dr. Charles Berger, a veterinarian. Charley lives in Thetford, Vermont, and specializes in the study of wolves and other large predators—although wild wolves have been extinct in Vermont since the early 1900's.

John Harris, the jolly man who shrinks from going up on that stage but walks nonchalantly among the wolves, has conquered his reluctance with astounding success. He and his wolves have driven more than a hundred thousand miles—halfway to the moon, or four times around the world, if you want to draw comparisons—and he will go to any lengths for the comfort and safety of his charges.

Three girls in California get to know the timber wolf, not as the arch child-terrifier of folklore, but as an affectionate playmate. (PHOTO BY ED SIMPSON, SOUTH PASADENA, CALIFORNIA)

More than once, for instance, in spite of the protests of their own children, a flying wedge of irate parents has met with city fathers and ousted John and his wolves. This warm and hospitable man has been forced to move seven times. He gets annoying telephone calls and abusive letters. He has even gone to jail twice because of someone else's prejudices.

In June of 1973, right in the middle of a New York City Neighborhood Houses Fair, Clem and Jethro were officially arrested. They were impounded by the authorities on the basis of a complaint lodged with the Department of Health. Watching them go were hundreds of stunned children, from whose embrace they had literally been torn only moments before.

"I didn't know what to do," John Harris told me. "We were supposed to lock them up because the law defined them as 'fierce and dangerous.' So we put them in cages in a private zoo—those fine animals that had never been behind bars in their lives."

He shook his head slowly at the memory of it. "So, you see," he said softly, "there's lots of educating left to do, yet."

Shortly after his brush with the law, John took Clem and Jethro out for a new round of visits. Pamela Innes wrote me a chatty letter a few days later. "Jethro and Clem are due to be at a fund-raising show," she said, "and then they have some movie and television appearances later in the week. It's a busy time for all of us."

The recollection of that unfortunate affair in New York City began to fade. One day, scarcely a month after the dangerous beasts had been imprisoned for the safety of all mankind, John went out to his van to give a last-minute pat to Clem and Jethro before driving off to their next appearance.

No friendly whines greeted his voice. No pink tongues smeared the window glass. No tails were raised, wagging in a welcoming salute. Clem and Jethro sprawled lifeless on the floor of their van. Trusting all humans to the last, they had accepted poisoned food from a stranger.

Clem was four years old at the time of his death. Jethro was seven. They had been good troupers in the finest tradition of show business—making as many as six appearances a day. They had endured hardships, improper food away from home, chilly trips in the back of the van, makeshift quarters while they awaited their cue to go on stage. Through it all they had helped John Harris, in their unspoken but eloquent way, to carry his urgent message of concern for the land and its wild creatures.

Clem and Jethro reached millions of persons with that message. But it wasn't quite enough. When word of their destruction burst on the national news services, their many sorrowing friends wished the message could have reached that vindictive one person more.

John Harris was racked with grief and self-condemnation. Pamela Innes sent me a note just hours after the death of the two wolves. Her usually perfect grammar collapsed under the weight of the tragedy. "We are not now what to do," her pen blurted on the postcard. "But we will go ahead somehow!"

Indeed, they did go ahead. As if by premonition, they had occasionally taken two wolf pups on tour with Clem and Jethro. Mariah and Rocky, the pups, were half-groomed for the job that Clem and Jethro had done. Now, suddenly, they had to grow up. On the last day of July, 1973, shortly after the murders, Pamela penned the following note and sent it to me:

"To everyone whose lives were touched
    by Jethro and Clem
We thank you.
And to everyone whose lives were not touched
    by these more than friendly and affectionate lives,
We are sorry."

Then she turned to the little female wolf:

"To Mariah—one of our new wolf puppies who travelled for
3 weeks on Jethro and Clem's last tour.
And you
little one, spared
with so little knowledge
of the 2 before you,
in whose footsteps
you will follow.
You loved them
and I can see it in your eyes
that you miss the love and affection that they
    showered on you.
In the short time
you had
with your pack
The lonely cry
you share with me
and the hurt we share together.
                    Pamela Innes

And how have Rocky and Mariah made out in their new
role? It was Rocky who was with us at Castleton State College, here in Vermont. At this writing he is only a year and a
half old, so he is still a pup, even though his eighty-five
pounds proclaim him almost at full adult weight. But he is all
wolf: golden-brown eyes, alert rounded ears, thick gray fur,
long legs, gaily waving tail.

Rocky is brought on stage after the showing of a magnificent film, *Death of a Legend*, produced by John Munro. In
this film the wolf appears in his true colors as the result of a
three-year photographic effort. His intense loyalty to his kind
is shown, along with the complicated communication system

by which the hierarchy of the pack is maintained from the dominant leader to tail-end Charlie.

The wolf's strange mixture of courage and shyness is shown in *Death of a Legend*, too—and Rocky proves it, right after the film. Prancing down the aisle and up onto the stage with John Harris, he is the picture of robust good health. Children pat him along the way, receiving that inevitable lick in return. His eyes miss nothing: every move, every outstretched arm, every gesture. Sometimes there are eight or ten hands petting him at once; he acknowledges them all.

Then comes the shyness part. Despite John Harris's admonition to speak quietly and make no sudden motion, someone always drops a pocketbook or slams a folding chair. Rocky, still new in the ways of a human crowd, recoils as if struck. That expressive tail disappears between his legs. He presses apprehensively against John's side. And if the audience breaks into spontaneous applause—as it did in Castleton that night— the sudden sound of nearly three hundred pairs of hands clapping is almost shattering in its effect on the wolf.

"He'll get over·it, though," smiles Harris. And, so well does this affable man know his wolves, you share his confidence that Rocky's stage fright is only temporary.

John welcomes the inevitable question: Why is this splendid animal kept in captivity? John raised Rocky from infancy, we are reminded: Rocky knows no life apart from man. "He just might romp up to the first campsite he saw," John chuckles. "Even though there is no authenticated instance of wolves making unprovoked attacks on humans, how would you feel if this fellow jumped out of the bushes and asked for a hamburger?"

Then, too, there is no such thing as a lone wolf—not in the normal wolf social structure, anyway. In the wild, Rocky would doubtless try to join a pack. However, lacking as he is in the fine graces of wild-reared animals, he'd probably not be accepted. Most packs are composed of family or near-relative groups, anyway—a structure he'd find hard to crack. His own parents are dead; so is his uncle, the unfortunate Jethro.

Rocky and Mariah will probably spend their lives with John Harris. In his care, their educational value is tremendous. This was plain after the show we attended in Vermont, when excited youngsters and adults alike wonderingly told each other that they had actually touched a real, live wolf.

John has a higher purpose than merely helping people to understand wolves, however. To him the predatory animal of any species is tied to its surroundings in an intricate way. It represents a single crossing of many skeins in a complex web that includes all living things. Pluck one strand and the entire structure vibrates. Destroy a strand as sturdy and vital as the wolf, and you threaten the collapse of the whole.

Harris's many friends in the United States and Canada helped him found the North American Association for the Preservation of Predatory Animals, of which he is president. NAAPPA's offices are at 13 Columbus Avenue, San Francisco, 94111. Interest in the organization soared with the death of Clem and Jethro, and contributions poured in from all over the continent. The Jethro Fund, 1201 Avenue K, Brooklyn, New York 11230, has been set up to help continue the work begun by the great Canadian wolf. Through another newly-formed group, Wolf Associates, at the same address, one may buy sweatshirts featuring Aleta Pahl's marvelous drawings of a wolf or a cheetah. Thus the influence of Clem and Jethro stretches far beyond their own lives.

In spite of the new understanding of the role of the predator that they convey in their talks, John Harris and Dr. Berger are quick to point out that you cannot easily replace the traditional Big, Bad Wolf with a new Big, Good Wolf. "A wolf—or any predator—goes about his business with deadly seriousness," they tell their audiences. "This is what makes him so efficient. If he botches the job, he'll drop out of the picture. The successful hunt is just as much a matter of life and death for him and his family as it is for his prey."

But early impressions die hard. People can recite the tale of Little Red Riding Hood and the Three Little Pigs as well after an evening with Harris and *Death of a Legend* as they could before they met those likeable wolves. Clem and Jethro—or, now, Rocky and Mariah—are great as individuals, it is true. But how about the pack that *does* race across the frozen tundra? What of the mountain lion that crouches on the ledge above the unsuspecting deer? They have been cast as the bad guys for most of us since childhood. Can John Harris make a single statement that the audience can take home as evidence that the predator is beneficial, even vital, to the health and well-being of its prey?

John answers the question with one of his own. It's a question that cuts to the core of the controversy that has raged ever since the first caveman found that he and a sabretooth tiger were after the same buffalo: If the predator, unchecked, is such a peril to the existence of its prey, how is it that pioneers in the New World found fish, birds and game beyond their dreams—when the predators had had their own way for centuries?

After he has posed this question, the smiling John Harris scratches the ears of one of his wolves. Then he strokes the rich fur, beginning at the expressive face and ending at the equally expressive brush at its nether end.

CHAPTER FIVE

Your Litter
or Your Life!

SHE'S JUST A LITTLE THING, and it
looked like a gigantic truck, but for Bobbie Kay Childers that
made the contest all the more exciting. "After all," she told
me, "anybody can put up a fuss when they see one candy
wrapper thrown out a car window. But how often can you
zero in on a whole truckload?"

Bobbie Kay lives in a little town in Arkansas. It's a lumber-
ing town, and much of the land is owned by the local paper
company. The company builds roads leading from the woods
to the mill where the logs are turned into paper and cardboard. When the cutting operation is finished the roads
remain, apparently leading nowhere. The company maintains
them, however, for fire control and access to other parts of its
extensive holdings. Such little-used areas become dumping
grounds for rubbish when nobody is looking.

"But *I* was looking," Bobbie Kay said. "I live near one of
those roads, and on a Saturday afternoon I saw a farm truck
go past the house. It was loaded to the top with old boards
and rusty metal and all sorts of junk. 'I bet he's taking that
stuff out to dump it,' I told myself.

"So I hopped in my car and took off after him. Sure

58

enough, he turned down what we call the southwest pike. These gravel roads are dusty most of the time, so it was no problem to follow him without being right on his tail."

Finally, as Bobbie Kay knew it would, the road came to an end. "And there he was," she said, "just backing his truck into the brush by the side of the road when I hove into sight. I pulled my car up to within about fifty feet of him and stopped."

The driver stared at Bobbie Kay. Then he busied himself with his sun visor, apparently adjusting something overhead. She watched him for a while, then got out and walked over to him. "I was shivering in my boots," she said. "He looked awful rough, and the truck window was so high that I could hardly look in. But I told myself I had gone this far, so I might's well keep going.

" 'You were going to dump that stuff here, weren't you?' I asked him. 'Oh, no, Ma'am,' he said. 'I was just looking around and enjoying the woods.' And he began to look this way and that, like a birdwatcher."

Bobbie Kay grinned sheepishly. "I don't know what came over me at that point, but I was getting mad. I had plenty to do back at the house, and here was this man wasting my whole afternoon. So I took the bull by the horns. 'I don't believe you,' I told him. 'In fact, I think you are a liar. You were going to dump your trash and you know it.' "

The frontal attack must have disarmed him. "No, Ma'am," he repeated. "Just enjoying the scenery."

"Well," she snapped, "so am I, then!" She flounced back to her car and began a little birdwatching on her own.

There the two of them sat, enjoying the scenery at the end of a dusty road. "But I told myself I could wait as long as he could," Bobbie Kay said, "and bigosh, I did!"

Fifteen minutes passed, then half an hour. It was the trucker who finally gave up. Jerking his vehicle into gear, he showered gravel all over Bobbie Kay as he headed back to town. She followed his dust trail in grim satisfaction, and even headed him off at one corner so she was waiting as he came down the road.

"And I followed him all the way to town," she said. "I still don't know why he didn't beat my brains out back there on the road, or at least dent my fender with his old truck. But I guess he didn't expect quite so much from someone no bigger than me."

Did she prevent that load from being jettisoned at some future date—perhaps an hour after their little birdwatching expedition? "Of course not," she said. "He just got rid of it somewhere else. But he knows I got his number, for what good that'll do. And I didn't just let him get away with the whole thing. At least I registered my protest."

Bobbie Kay Childers has been known to do more than just register protest, however. This willowy housewife, who weighs in at "a hundred pounds when I'm carrying a bag of groceries," sometimes gets riled enough to make a phone call to Janice Clark. Then things begin to happen.

"This is your garbage lady again," Bobbie Kay says. "I've found an interesting little display out on Lone Pine Road. Let me know when you'd be able to take a look at it. And don't forget your camera."

Camera-toting Janice Clark writes for the Crossett, Arkansas, *News-Observer*. Together she and Bobbie Kay photograph the offending batch of rubbish; then they carefully pick the pile apart, piece by piece. Soon they identify the culprit through a series of clues: a magazine label here, a discarded envelope there.

Janice has a regular section in the *News-Observer*. "They've been just great at the paper," she told me. "They give me a page every Thursday. And I make sure I use every inch of it."

And use it she does. Janice pulls no punches. "Is This Your Litter?" she asks under one picture. "This truckload of litter

Janice Clark examines a roadside litter dump near Crossett, Arkansas, for clues to where the litter came from. With a few able colleagues, Janice attempts to lead local litterbugs to mend their ways.

was deposited on Waterwell Road, along the woodland approach to a number of attractive homes in the area. The wedding packages and other addressed material made it easily identifiable as having belonged to a young couple who were moving into a new home in Crossett."

Then comes the clincher: "Would that couple like to have to see this mess every time they approached their home?" Apparently not. Two days after the large photograph appeared, the litter had vanished.

Beside another picture of a discarded loafer, the caption admonishes: "If the Shoe Fits—Wear It!!" Charitably—"and because I have to live in this town, too"—Janice refrains from actually naming the guilty parties. "But they know who they are," she says. "And they know that I know, too. I remember one time when I went back to look at a mess I'd photographed for the paper. It was picked up, raked, and even swept clean. But what got me was a little sign they'd stuck right in the middle of the spot. It had one word on it: *Thanks*."

It's little personal triumphs like these that keep Janice cheerfully on her busy way. "I've had to jump over dead cows and dead goats," she recalls, "and I have ruined my hose climbing in trash. Once I had to come back and bathe and spray and freshen up before the school board meeting."

And what about Bobbie Kay Childers, ferreting out somebody else's mistakes—does she feel like an informer? "Not at all," she told me, her eyes flashing. "The way I feel when I see something that should be cleared up is that I'm a little guilty, too, if I just let it lie there."

Bobbie Kay—and Janice—have their counterparts all across the continent, we discovered. Peg and I sat talking with Dr. Gerry Kremer and his wife, Joan, of Winnipeg, Manitoba. As we chatted, a car drove past us and a beverage can arched out of the window and went clattering down the street half a block away. Without a word, Gerry got up and trotted off after the offending container. Then he brought it back and set it down beside his chair.

In response to our unspoken question, he smiled. "When that clod tossed the can out, it was his litter," he said, "but as soon as I heard it hit the street it became mine."

This put me in mind of a city dweller we visited in Providence, Rhode Island. He lived in one of a whole street of look-alike homes on the edge of town. At first glance, about the only difference between his house and those on either side was the color of his awnings. As we sat on his tiny front porch I asked the inevitable question: How was he sure he'd have the right house when he got in late at night?

"Nothing to it," he quipped. "I just walk along the curb until I'm not kicking any more cans and bottles. Then I know I'm home."

I looked out into the street. Sure enough, the pavement in front of his house did not boast so much as a cigarette butt. "You clean it once," he said, "and it's no problem to keep it that way. But if everybody else on the street cleans up his forty feet, too, I'm really in trouble. I won't know my own house any more."

Incidentally, my friend has an interesting idea for cleaning up roadsides and sidewalks. "Simple," he says. "Just make everybody responsible for the trash in front of his own place. When I lived in New York City I had to shovel the snow off my sidewalk or pay a fine. I couldn't throw the snow out into the street, either. If I did, I might pay *two* fines."

The initial cleanup campaign, he conceded, would be a mess, as everybody headed for the disposal site with trunk-loads of litter. We added helpfully that people without cars would have to haul stuff away in wheelbarrows and toy wagons. Probably they wouldn't do it at all. But that was all right, too, he told us; their fines would finance a whole fleet of pickup vans—plus the men to run them.

"Anyway," he said, "this puts the problem right where it belongs: on the shoulders of the guy who tossed the junk in the first place. As things stand now, about the only deterrent is the rare instance when he gets caught. It's usually up to somebody else to pick up after him—a bunch of kids, for instance, out to clean up a mess that's none of their own doing at all."

This, we admitted, was often the case, yet we took heart in the thought that these young people would be the adults of tomorrow, with new ideals, new standards. "And no matter who picks it up," Peg added, "it's largely the adults who foot the bill."

Not always is it old *vs.* young, anyway. Scoutmasters, 4-H officials, youth leaders know what a joy it can be to work with youngsters. Then, too, the kids can get things started all by themselves.

I remember, for instance, a busload of school children we once saw on an outing. The bus stopped at a hamburger stand where we were having a snack, and half a hundred children poured out. Busloads of children, of course, are scarcely new, and I hardly gave them more than a glance until I realized what they were doing. Chattering and laughing, the children were picking up as much litter as they could carry from around the stand and its parking area. They took the litter to their bus, where several trash bags had been brought out for the occasion.

Within five minutes, before our astonished eyes, that parking lot had been picked clean. Impressed, I walked over to their teacher. "I'm interested," I began. "In fact, I'm flabbergasted at how those kids worked this place over. Is this some kind of conservation class?"

To my surprise, he looked sheepish. "Well," he replied, "I'll tell you if you promise not to laugh."

I assured him that anybody who could channel such exuberance into a blitz on litter would get no ridicule from me. "You'd never guess it," he said, "but we're a history class."

"A *history* class?"

"That's right. We're on our way from Boston to visit Fort Ticonderoga. We saved up all year for this trip. Made fudge, sold Christmas cards, had food sales. A couple of our kids even found an old orchard and peddled a lot of knobby apples."

While I wondered how apples and Christmas cards related to rest-stop rehabilitation, he went on. "One of the things we tried to find out was how the Ticonderoga countryside looked back in Revolutionary War days," he said. "In fact, we made a little table display of the scene, using toy buildings and trees made of sprigs of moss. When one kid jokingly suggested we ought to scatter a few bottles and cans around to make it look real, the others jumped on him. So the boy, as much in self-defense as anything, said he bet Ticonderoga *would* look like that today. Besides, if they thought it was so funny, were they prepared to clean it up if he was right?"

The class rose to the bait. They decided, however, that the entire fort was too big a task to tackle. But they had become interested, so they agreed to clean up the next best thing: any roadside area where they stopped on their way to the fort. And so a snack bar in Middlebury, Vermont "looked just like Ticonderoga," as one youngster, boarding the bus again, remarked to his satisfaction. And when the children reached the fort, they must have realized that their spotless parking area was, indeed, nearly as clean as the well-kept *Place d'Armes* of that honored citadel.

So the point is being made, here and there. And since this particular idea started with the children themselves, it may stay with them long after they forget how to spell "Ticonderoga."

A snack bar was also the target of a juvenile cleanup we ran into clear out in Hawaii. Peg and I were visiting my brother when we saw an unusual article in the Hilo *Tribune-Herald*, where Jim is a reporter. Intrigued by the contents of the article, I telephoned across the island to a McDonald's stand, on the Kona Coast, where the cleanup was to take place. I asked Jack Woods, the manager, about the unusual activity that was planned. Where did he get such an idea, anyway?

"Well, it started as an Easter egg hunt to advertise our restaurant," Jack said. "We planned the hunt several weeks in advance. We put out lots of publicity on the radio and in the papers, and we had about three hundred children signed up. The idea was that they'd search for the eggs on the grounds around our restaurant. We'd have prizes and awards and all the usual fanfare.

"I was thinking about it as I drove to work one morning," he continued. "As I got within a few blocks of the restaurant, a napkin fluttered across the road. 'That's a McDonald's napkin,' I told myself. Then I saw another. And the closer I got to the stand the more plastic spoons and straws and throwaway junk I saw. And most of it, I had to admit, I recognized right away."

I heard him chuckle over the phone. "Then a thought hit me all of a sudden: Now, wait a minute, Woods—you've got three hundred kids signed up to look for eggs. That's three hundred little backs bent over, and three hundred little pairs of hands reaching for something to grab. What if each of them grabbed a handful of trash?"

Since prizes were to be awarded anyway, how about adding a rule that the contestants had to pick up the dregs with the eggs? Something like "No Litter, No Loot," perhaps, or "No Trash—No Treasure?"

The more Jack Woods thought about it the better it seemed. "Litter is a sensitive spot with any snack bar worth its salt," he quipped, "and here was a chance to do something about it."

There was only a week to go, but Jack Woods is young and resourceful. He paid a personal visit to the offices of the Hilo *Tribune-Herald*. "Right across from our place it's a mess," he admitted as he gave out the latest details of the hunt, "and this will help us clean it up."

Local radio and television went along with the refurbished rules. "What's new on McDonald's farm?" asked one announcer. "Three hundred knee-high farmhands, that's what!"

When I first talked with Jack Woods it was Good Friday morning. The egg hunt was to take place the following day and I had an appointment on the opposite side of the island. But we got together again on the phone late the next afternoon. "How'd it go?" I asked.

There was silence on the other end of the line. But just for a moment. Then I realized what the silence meant: Jack was trying to find the right words.

"I can't believe it!" he exulted. "I just can't believe it! Not only did they clean up that trashy Sarona Road, but they kept right on going. They went farther than where the eggs were hidden, but it didn't seem to matter. They went clear to the traffic barrier signs the county put across the road. The whole place isn't just picked up—it sparkles!"

Half in jest, half in earnest, I asked about the long-term effects of the campaign. Did he really believe the new look would be permanent?

"Oh, I don't think so," he admitted. "It's true that it probably won't last. But then—neither does a bath."

Since follow-up seemed pretty important, I got in touch with Jack Woods later in the summer, when the exhilaration of the hunt should have long been forgotten. But there was more follow-up than either of us had counted on. "The cleanup drive seemed to kick off a large campaign around the entire community," he told me. "And my company has authorized me to purchase a small vehicle to use for roadside cleanup."

But there was still more. "The most important thing that has come from the cleanup is now that it's clean, people seem to notice and help keep it cleaner. This is not to say that it doesn't get dirty again, but it is staying much cleaner than ever before."

The idea of teaching by example is scarcely new, of course. It works as well around a New England town as at a restaurant in Hawaii. "Try it yourself," suggests Alberta Reynolds, a kindergarten teacher we met in Nashua, New Hampshire. "We take the children out around the school grounds on nice days. When I see a bit of junk—even a gum wrapper or the pull ring from a soft drink can—I pick it up. Pretty soon I've got the boys and girls doing the same thing. And not a word has been said. Sometimes I remind myself of a mother hen pecking at seeds to show her chicks what's good for them. Only in this case I'm pointing out the not-so-good."

Litter-picking may go back to prehistoric days when ancient man piled his shells and bones in heaps near the campfire. Only recently have massive campaigns such as Keep Canada Green, Earth Day and, here in Vermont, Green-Up Day become a part of the scene. These are massive bandwagon efforts, with plenty of fanfare. The average person lacks the skill, money and time to carry out any such sustained drive. Understandably, he takes mental stock of himself and says, "But I'm just one small person—what can *I* do?"

Teenage Keith Armstrong of Buffalo, New York, asked himself that question, too. He noted a couple of areas near his house that seemed to collect more than their share of trash. To make things worse, there was not a garbage can in sight. Knowing that roadside junk is self-perpetuating, the first bit of trash inviting more, Keith cleaned up the areas.

"Then the question was how to keep them looking clean," he told us as we chatted with him at his family's lakeside cottage. "I could put a couple of rubbish barrels there, of course, but unless I chained them down I figured they'd get stolen."

After some thought, he decided to give the barrels a little personality. He painted a message on the side of each of them. One bore the instructions For Your Petty Trash, another, Your Litter Or Your Life!

The idea worked. "Apparently it appealed to people's sense of humor," he chuckled. "They were good about using those barrels. Too good, in fact. After the first week I needed a dozen barrels instead of just a couple."

Keith's private campaign suffered from an embarrassment of riches—if you want to use that fancy term for the raw material he collected—and he looks forward to the day when he can, indeed, have the dozen barrels he needs. "Maybe a whole trainload, Mr. Rood. And a fleet of trucks to pick 'em up daily."

Perhaps Keith Armstrong's success was due to the way he tickled the funnybones of Buffalo's litterbugs. Apparently, litterbugs elsewhere find a sense of humor intriguing, too. Put Your Trash Into Orbit . . . Five Minutes says a sign along a roadside in Manitoba. Drive five minutes longer and you discover a white sphere four feet in diameter with a gaping hole in its side. Then you understand what the sign meant; the sphere is really a fiberglass litter barrel. On it is the single word: *Orbit.*

Nor is that all. Next to Orbit is a smaller container on a post. A glance at the container shows it to be a dispenser of trash bags. Toss your litter into Orbit, yank out a fresh bag, and you're on your way.

How has Orbit worked out in practice? Better, apparently, than threatening signs that admonish the traveler against littering, according to the Manitoba Highways Department Traffic Section.

"In the first two years [since Orbit was introduced in 1964] our highway maintenance forces reported definite decreases in the amount of litter along the highways," says the Department. "The space theme has added interest to the program and the soft-sell approach was instituted by erecting those signs directing motorists to 'Put Your Trash Into Orbit,' with the distance to the orbit indicated in minutes and seconds in the manner of a count down."

Peter Boychuk, Signs Technician, told me that public reaction had been most gratifying. The Department had received many favorable comments about the container "and about the riddle aspect of the methods of signing as well as the orbit idea itself."

Motorists in British Columbia are invited to feed the Garbage Gobbler. This insatiable critter is really a barrel surrounded by a fiberglass shell shaped something like an owl with an open mouth. Michael Pope, Senior Landscape Supervisor, notes that children are always ready to feed the gobbler. However, as with Keith Armstrong's lettered litter barrels, the device attracts almost too much attention. "They [the Gobblers] were adequate from the first in small parks or picnic areas, but for highway litter stops additional containers had to be used," Pope told me.

Anyone who travels in Canada soon realizes that, even in large cities such as Winnipeg, Ottawa and Montreal, the streets are far cleaner than their counterparts in the United States. Part of this happy circumstance is due, doubtless, to Canada's smaller population. Much of it, however, stems from the Canadian's deep pride in the beauty and cleanliness of his country. He respects it and appreciates it. His roadside litter campaigns help to keep his land as he knows it should be.

At Peterborough, Ontario, I enthused about the Dominion's clean countryside to my friend Doug Sadler, who writes a conservation column for the Peterborough *Examiner*. "Well," Doug agreed, "we like to think we're trying. Here in

Peterborough you've got to give credit to the Golden Garbage Can."

This notable container, I discovered, is awarded annually to the school doing the best job of cleaning up streets and roadsides in the school-grounds area. Radio stations, television and newspapers join with local merchants in publicizing the campaign.

It is part of Conservation Week, sponsored each June by the Otonabee Region Conservation Authority, and the Pollution Probe of Peterborough. There are kite-flying and fly-tying contests, poster contests, free movies, a public picnic and a gigantic cleanup free-for-all.

Some surprising "finds" have turned up in the all-out efforts to win the trophy: an old automobile, for instance, exhumed from its supposed final resting place and brought in by triumphant and strong-backed students. Other treasures have included a transistor radio that played, an abandoned canoe that floated, and a forgotten car battery that didn't do anything. One student thoughtfully slipped a snake into a girl's litterbag. Another cleaned up the area he had covered the year before—and found his old leather work gloves.

Peg and I were a few days too early to watch the Peterborough campaign in progress, but we asked Sandra Kelly of the Otonabee Conservation Authority about it later. The actual cleanup, we learned, is done by schools. Each school area is looked at before, during and after the campaign. "In this way the judges can achieve a relative cleanup viewpoint," she told us.

Since evaluation of areas is on a before-and-after basis, the size of any particular school is of little importance to the merit of its cleanup. Thus, although the prize one year went to three hundred students in the seventh and eighth grades of the Adam Scott school, it had been presented the year before to the eighty-nine students of Parkhill Public School. The students of this little school had thus bested more than five thousand other students—and adults—and walked off with the Golden Garbage Can.

Litter campaigns, of course, are familiar in the United States as well as in Canada. As in Peterborough, some of our schools let their students out on cleanup drives for an entire school day, thus giving extra importance to the idea of cleanup. Often the press and local businesses will lend encouragement and support. They may provide litter bags, collection trucks, and even a banquet at the end of the day.

As with nearly everything involving real live people, there's the human side to consider. There will always be snags. One of the hardest working 4-H groups we know is under the leadership of Mrs. John Hellerich of Good Thunder, Minnesota. Her Lyra Merryworkers have a dozen different projects going on most of the time. However, even youthful energy can sometimes get bogged down—as happened during one of the club's recent cleanup efforts.

A group of boys had been sent out to pick up litter along the roadside. Sometime later a truck went to collect the bags of trash they had gathered. The truck found the line of bags along the roadside, all right, but there was no group of boys at the end of it.

Perplexed, one of the adults began a careful check along the route near the last bag. Sure enough, there were the boys—down behind a bush, huddled over something they had discovered by the side of the road. It was an old copy of *Playboy*.

A garden club near Columbia, South Carolina undertook its own little roadside cleanup. In the process, one of the members found a quarter in the sand. This gave them an idea; they "salted" the roadbanks with a few dollars' worth of coins from the club treasury. Then they let it be known that it just might be profitable for people to hike along town roads, litterbag in hand. Result: everybody had fun, the roadsides were scoured—and several lucky prospectors struck it rich.

There are hilltop cleanups, valley cleanups, park and beach and forest cleanups. Scores of school and college classes, each of which would be mentioned here by name if space permitted, are waging constant war against litter. Their efforts range from picking up junk on the area around the president's mansion (we actually saw this taking place at a small college in Georgia) to a "wade-in" that netted tons of old metal, plastic and glass from a rejuvenated river near Chicago.

The Granite State Scubadivers have an Underwater Cleanup Day in Nashua, New Hampshire, each year. So does a skindiving club near Minneapolis. One of the divers in this latter group was cruising around through the murk of the waters of the river when he spotted an old auto tire. Upon looking closer he noticed some raised printing on the wall of the tire.

Inflate To 70 Pounds, the printing read. Such air pressures have not been used in auto tires for fifty years or more. So, quite likely, that bit of litter had been resting there since the days of the Model T. Two generations later, something was being done about it.

Our preoccupation with the automobile, even in these days of gasoline shortages, has led us to produce what might be called on-the-run litter. This caters to one of America's favorite pastimes—tossing things out car windows. At the exit to several service areas on interstate highways, the motorist sees a sign, Please Don't Litter—Toss It Here! The sign indicates a rubbish barrel with a funnel-shaped opening so the traveler can toss his trash on the run.

We've noted similar devices on the open highway, too. Once we saw a carload of youngsters career past one such area at high speed, bombarding it with a fusillade of cans and bottles. Of course most of the junk missed the basket, but the Highway Department evidently felt it was better to have rubbish scattered over a few hundred feet than strewn over miles of highway.

Doubtless our roadways and waterways would be in much worse condition but for the efforts of tens of thousands of individuals, Saturday afternoon groups, parent-and-children combinations, all of whom make cleanliness their personal concern. Most of us have seen such people along roadsides as we drove by.

I wish we could somehow extend our gratitude to all these people. They seldom receive any thanks—nor do they expect any. Conscious of the thousands I must omit in this account, I'll close the chapter with a few words about Anne Pugsley.

Anne lives in the Forest Park section of Oklahoma City. As with so many other teenagers today, she was appalled at the sight of local streets, roads, and nearby Interstate 35. With characteristic youthful directness she tramped out onto those streets, bag in hand, and started her own cleanup campaign.

Anne got two friends to help her; together they picked up tons of throw-aways over an entire summer. The pure trash went to the dump in the car of her father, Dr. William Pugsley. Beer and soft drink cans went to a collection center.

People driving to work day after day looked with interest at the sight of these teenagers. Their reactions varied from an irritated blast of the horn to a friendly toot. But the response of one motorist was quite unexpected.

When he spied the girls, he drew his car to a stop. Pulling alongside Anne, he opened the car door and got out. He reached into the car seat and extracted a sack of trash.

Walking over to the dumfounded girl, he pulled open her large litter bag and in it deposited his sack.

Then, with a nod of greeting and a sunny smile, he drove away.

CHAPTER SIX

Garbage into Gold

THE RANGER AT BIG BEND National Park contemplated a bit of white paper fluttering from a low bush. "And that, ladies and gentlemen," he assured us, "is a genuine Kleenex plant."

He snapped the twig that bore the flimsy banner. Then he held it up for all to see. "The Kleenex plant used to be pretty rare in these parts. Then it got downright common. But lately we're seeing less of it. Perhaps we're going to recover from the Throwaway Syndrome, after all."

This disease—the Throwaway Syndrome—is familiar to us all. When you suffer from it you can carry a heavy six-pack, full, up the face of a mountain, but once it's empty and light you cannot bring it down again. You can drive the family gas-buggy halfway to the moon, but you cannot limp it out of town to its grave at the landfill.

The malady can strike at any moment. The hotdog you order bears more frills than a pampered pooch in a penthouse. It's diapered in leakproof paper, cradled in a cardboard "boat" and blanketed in a toss-out napkin. Extra goodies may include little squeeze packets of mustard, ketchup and relish. If you order take-out coffee, there's the cup and cover, stick, envelopes of bogus cream and sugar—all in a paper bag. The flint-shelled coconut at the grocery store is shrouded in the same flimsy plastic wrap as the overripe plum.

For years such nonedibles were tossed away without a second thought. Now, however, we just may save that tissue for an extra sniff. We may carry a litter-bag (a word unknown a generation ago) in the car, and even shop around for the best deal among local junkyards when the old bus finally wheezes its last.

One reason for the decrease in the Throwaway Syndrome is the practical one of personal economics. With nearly everything costing more, you may save assorted plastic bags to be used again, for instance—instead of capering over the landscape, flinging them as a nymph tosses roses. Besides, if you're caught, you're fined. And why not get forty bucks for your old car after it expires? Certainly you paid enough for it.

Another reason, doubtless, for the subtle change in the landscape that the Big Bend ranger detected is the impact of such programs as Keep America Beautiful, Johnny Horizon and Woodsy Owl. We are becoming aware that maybe we are, indeed, a little flip—so to speak—in the way we dispose of disposables: that, in a sense, we are wasting our waste.

Not all of us find this to be a great revelation, of course. My father has had a compost heap ever since I can remember. He feeds it daily rations of grapefruit peel, coffee grounds and eggshells. When the first kitchen sink garbage disposer came on the market, he allowed as how he wondered what anybody'd put in it. Many a housewife has saved paper bags, egg boxes and old string for years. And, in a piece of low comedy that now shows a grain of truth, the scribbled instructions on the wall of a men's room near the Mississippi River urge the user: "Flush Quick—they need it downstream."

Peter Tonge of the *Christian Science Monitor* recently sent me a fascinating booklet titled "Garbage Into Gold." The booklet contained a number of articles he had written on how people had learned to use much of the material we commonly class as junk. It showed how they did, indeed, turn clutter into cash—or, at least, put it to money-saving uses.

Peg and I saw garbage turned into gold in a number of places on our trip. My journal includes notes on a variety of once-agains: the teacher in Phoenix, for instance, who had a rack draped with paper towels at the back of her room, each towel labeled with a student's name. She made her class spread the towels out to dry after using. We saw "stone walls" made of bottles, plastic jugs fashioned into scoops, bowls and bird feeders.

We were guests of a thrifty Utah couple who had found a use for old magazines—they wrapped them around their hot water pipes in the cellar for insulation. We were told of an Illinois poultryman who insulated the walls of his home with feathers, just as Benjamin Franklin once had done. We ate out of coconut-shell bowls in Hawaii that my nieces had made, and drank from cut-off beer bottle tumblers in Nevada.

In Toronto we were shown a large household freezer filled with dozens of quart milk cartons containing home-frozen food.

"We freeze our leftovers, too," Patty Albert told us, pointing to several TV-dinner trays. "We keep these trays on hand for the purpose. Add a little meat, a few vegetables, some dessert anytime they're extra. Freeze the trays when they're full, and reheat them some day when you're short of time. This makes it unnecessary to keep picking at a roast, for instance, until everybody's sick of it."

Her husband chuckled. "Sure does. And it adds up to the darndest meals you ever saw. Where else can you get scallops with a side order of chocolate sauce?"

These days everybody, it seems, has rediscovered the old-timer's practice of "use it up, wear it out, make it do." Hence, the Richard Pelsue family of Essex Center, Vermont, is right in style. Dick is a masonry contractor. He, his wife, Barbara, and their four children squeeze the last bit out of nearly everything that comes their way.

The Pelsues have the usual domestic animals you'd expect around a farm, plus a thrifty vegetable garden. Once a week Dick goes to the local bakery and brings back three bran sacks of stale bread. This, added to garbage provided by the Pelsues' neighbors, plus discarded produce from grocery stores, is willingly converted by the Pelsues' pigs into mini-cost pork. More scraps go to the chickens. In addition, the Pelsues' vegetables grow deep in organic material: you have to dig down quite a way to come to anything that would qualify as plain soil.

That garden, rich as it is, receives additional topdressing in the form of manure from a nearby farm, bark from a local lumberyard, and compost from the few table scraps that do not get processed into pork or poultry. In the spring Barbara spreads newspapers between the rows to discourage weeds. The paper eventually rots into the soil, providing nourishment. On top of the newspaper is a layer of hay, then a sprinkling of bark and wood chips. The feeling underfoot is that of walking on the rich humus of a deep forest.

Dick and Barbara Pelsue make careful use of almost every inch of their twenty-two acres. The raw material for their enterprise would be shortly dismissed by many people as garbage. Spread carefully on the land, however, and processed through its soil, its plants and animals, mere garbage brings the Pelsues handsome returns—aided, of course, by the good sun that makes it all go.

The good sun is put to more direct use by three men in Colorado. They have a new slant on the use of solar energy as a source of heat.

The men, Jim Peterson and Marc Thomsen of Boulder, and Jerry Plunkett of Denver, were featured in an article in the *Denver Post*. Their idea is based on a familiar principle: dark materials soak up the sun's warmth. Once the heat is absorbed

*In Lincoln, Vermont, refuse is bulldozed into a landfill. In fills, re-
cycling centers, and other projects can be seen an emphasis on dispos-
ing of waste in such a way that it is put to use.* (PHOTO BY MARGERY E.
SHARP)

it may be given off immediately, or it may be stored.

In this solar device, air is gently guided across an expanse of dark surface, which is placed on a steep sunny slope such as that of a roof or wall. The air emerges heated at the upper edge. Properly channeled, the men believe, it could heat a house.

That's the "gold" in this day of fuel shortages. Now where's the "garbage?" Simple: the heated surface is covered with beer cans—hundreds of them. The cans are cut off at about two inches, glued to a large square of plywood, and painted black. The plywood square, covered with the cans, looks like an enormous black honeycomb.

The plywood, with its attached cans, is placed approximately broadside to the sun's rays, but exact positioning is not critical. The round shape of the beer cans assures that they'll absorb plenty of energy no matter what the shifting angle of the sun.

Sounds simple enough, and it works. Dick Prouty, who reported in the *Post* on the invention, says a demonstration on a hazy afternoon boosted air from 60 to 140 degrees. A good Colorado sun would take that air to more than 200 degrees—almost enough to boil water.

The next question, of course, is just how large a gadget would be needed to heat a house. The three inventors haven't yet worked out the answer to that one; at this writing they are still testing it. One of their hopes is that, since houses vary in shape and location, a kit can be produced that will allow the home handyman to build his own solar heating plant. Six hundred square feet—the size of one side of a small roof—will require six thousand cans.

That's a lot of beer cans—*empty* beer cans—which, according to Dick Prouty, means the thirsty handyman can start assembling material for his project at once.

While Peterson, Thomsen and Plunkett count their beer cans

by the thousands, one of Plunkett's fellow townsmen takes his one at a time. Or at least that's how he started.

Roland Byberg of Denver worked as a railroad signal maintainer for thirty-eight years. When he retired he found little to occupy his time. One day, however, a friend gave his wife, Louise, a tiny chair that had been fashioned from an aluminum beer can. Byberg inspected it, thought a while, and set out to construct one like it.

"I decided it ought to be an easy item to make," he told me, "but it took me over five hours to make that first chair. However, I found something that not only interested me, but was fun as well."

To turn a beer can into a miniature chair, Roland first removes one end from the can. He then cuts the sides in thin strips down to the other end. Turned up, turned down, and twisted, these strips become the arms, legs and back of the chair, while the concave bottom of the can becomes the seat.

"This first design we dubbed the 'Antique Chair,' " Roland said. "We followed it with an original design we called the 'Fan Back,' because of its resemblance to an old-fashioned cane-back chair in an expansive fan shape.

"A chair by itself seems lonely, so then came a design for a cocktail table," he continued. "Short-legged cocktail tables became Ottoman footrests to go with the chairs. Louise decided to improve my chairs by spray painting them in wrought iron black, gold, white and silver. She also added foam rubber cushions covered with velvets and brocades of all colors.

"At this point we began to sell our chairs in great numbers, due primarily to Lou's innovations. Now we have as gifts and for sale several hundred individual chairs and sets of chairs, rockers and Ottomans."

Roland Byberg's chairs are great collector's items, doll furniture and just plain conversation pieces. One of his most ornate creations occupies an honored place on my mantel.

Dubbed the King Chair, its back is woven of metal strips, with fancy scrollwork at legs and arms, making it look like a throne. It is unpainted, so the brand name, *Coors*, can be deciphered on the strips. A while ago we had a visit from a friend of mine who has spent long years in the Vermont Highway Department. Curious as to what he'd say, I showed him that four-inch aluminum jewel.

He looked at it a few moments, hands clasped behind his back. Then he removed it from the mantel, inspected it carefully, replaced it and turned to me. "Ron," he said, doubtless thinking of the thousands of cans he had seen along roadsides during those long years in the highway truck, "that's the first beer can I ever saw that looks just great right where it is."

The name Coors, by the way, is borne by all of Roland Byberg's chairs—at least, until Louise hits them with the spray paint. Not that Roland is partial to the brand, necessarily, but Coors beer uses aluminum cans exclusively. Aluminum, Roland finds, is soft and easy to work. It is also valuable, a fact that has led the makers of Coors beer to do some thinking about the fate of the millions of Coors cans that do not find their way into Roland Byberg's hands.

The Adolph Coors Company, of Golden, Colorado, produces the top-selling beer in ten of the eleven far-western states where Coors is sold. Even non beer-drinkers were once Coors customers; during Prohibition days the company kept afloat, so to speak, by manufacturing malted milk. And, today, both drinkers and non-drinkers in still a third group bear the company in great respect. This group is composed of highway personnel, outdoor enthusiasts, people who appreciate roadside beauty. Coors, it seems, bears an enviable record in keeping its containers off the street.

The company has long been sensitive, as have most beverage manufacturers, to the adverse publicity of an empty can or bottle by the roadside. As far back as 1959, when Coors

introduced the seven-ounce aluminum beer container, it paid
a penny for each one returned.

Coors's can-return project was dropped for various reasons
in 1965, but taken up again in 1970. Now, with its seven-,
twelve- and sixteen-ounce containers, the Coors cash-for-
aluminum-cans program is in full swing, netting about five
million pounds of aluminum a month.

Aluminum beverage cans of any make can be turned in at
Coors collection centers located at strategic points over the
company's eleven-state sales area. Cans are paid for at the
rate of fifteen cents per pound. Half of all Coors cans are
returned to the company. In addition, Coors bottles are bought
at a penny each throughout the company's territory. The
cans are melted down by several large aluminum companies
and returned to Coors, which fills and seals its own cans.
Returned bottles may be reused or crushed and made into
new glass.

Even at fifteen cents a pound (about twenty-four aluminum containers), there's real cash in those cans. Coors paid
out nearly five million dollars for the return of empties in
1974. With aluminum lending itself so handily to repeated
reuse, it was worth it to the company, according to the
Coors representatives who answered our questions about the
cash-for-cans program.

Coors has found, then, that collection and reuse of old
containers makes good economic sense from the point of view
of production costs. And then, too, the company is not un-
aware of the publicity and advertising its product gets from
the hundreds of Coors collection centers broadcast all over
the West.

The can collection program also makes economic sense to
the tireless members of the Order of the Aching Back in
Coors's sales area. One husband-wife team turned in a whop-
ping quarter-million cans over a four-month period and won
a trip to the Super Bowl, according to the Coors publication,

Aluminews. The contest was sponsored by the Aluminum Company of America, which supplies some of the metal for Coors cans.

Other rewards, reported in *Aluminews,* have included more than a thousand dollars in can refunds for the Colorado Boys' Ranch at La Junta. Three times that amount has been collected for handicapped workers at Goodwill Industries of Denver. "Our church has sent several needy kids to camp on beer-can money," one clergyman said. "Our members just found the cans lying around," he hastened to assure me.

In the Grand Canyon State the Arizona Wholesale Beer and Liquor Association joined with the Arizona Soft Drink Bottlers Association to set up collection centers for cans and bottles. The name of the new project—well, what else? It's called The Beverage Industry Recycling Program—BIRP, for short.

Such large-scale operations as the Coors and Arizona collection programs count their proceeds in tons and in millions of dollars. Smaller efforts are taking place, too: the local scout troop that puts on a paper drive, the school that collects old magazines, and the garden club that sets up a bin at a shopping plaza where you can toss your cans and bottles. These little campaigns are as important, in their way, as the big ones, for it's the private user who ends up with much of the junk. He can put it back in circulation, if he will.

To single out the best school salvage programs among thousands, for instance, would be impossible, even if I had been able to visit them all. However, the students and faculty of the Rocky Mountain School of Carbondale, Colorado, are perhaps typical of the new attitude toward toss-outs.

Peg and I had been invited to visit the school as guests of Roo Wolcott. Roo is one of about a hundred students in the little private school; she had been a student of mine a few years earlier in Vermont.

She introduced me to Dick Herb, her biology teacher. Dick showed us around the grounds of the school—the brook where his classes foraged for aquatic life; the overgrown meadow, in which they knew the name of every weed and bush; the nearby peaks where they walked beside streams swollen with spring snows.

Our tour took us to a series of wooden bins at the back of the dining hall. One bin was for bottles; one for aluminum cans, one for other metal and one for cardboard.

"Here's our 'Think Twice' area," Dick said. "It's been in operation for two school years. The students are real excited about it; they co-operate even better than we had dared to hope. We handle a great deal of cans and cardboard and paper."

He reached into one bin and pulled out a cardboard box. "Landfill area studies show that cardboard accounts for nearly half the bulk of waste material when compacted. So to help our own little landfill, we try to save out as much cardboard as possible. Here in western Colorado, Safeway food stores will take all we can bring, bale it up and take it off our hands."

We asked Dick how such a program came out financially. "You know," he smiled, "we've become so money-oriented that the cash angle puzzled the students at first. They couldn't help but ask: 'You pile that cardboard into the truck, drive all the way to Safeway and they don't even *pay* you? No profit in that!'

"But that's part of these kids' education," he continued. "We make it clear that there are other things in life than money. Even where we *do* get paid for our trash, it's a losing proposition. Here we are, a school, with a couple of hundred people producing waste materials. Last year we put out more than two tons of paper, loaded it into a truck and took it away to be sold. We got twenty-five dollars for the whole load. This didn't even pay for the truck and driver."

At this point Roo Wolcott spoke up. "But think of two tons of waste that didn't provide all that bulk at the landfill, all that smoke from the incinerator or all that litter along the road."

With cans and metal the school just about broke even. And bottles? "Again you've got to count on something besides sheer economics," Dick said. "Our class studied about an asphalt plant that said it would take in all the bottles brought to it and grind them up for inclusion in road-building materials. So there was a massive local drive put on by residents, scouts, service clubs, church groups. They got a tremendous mountain of bottles.

"The asphalt plant took all the bottles, just as it had promised. The townspeople even used brooms and shovels to sweep up fragments. Then the plant mixed the glass into asphalt and used it for road building."

He paused to let Roo finish the story. "And do you know," she said, "how little asphalt they really produced? After all that effort, those weeks of collection, the news publicity, the storage, the cleanup? They paved only about a quarter mile of highway—what a car could drive over in fifteen seconds!"

But the important point was elsewhere. "I don't know what all that hard labor was worth at the going wage," said this high school junior, soon to take her place in the world, "but better those bottles under your car and useful for fifteen seconds than alongside it for fifteen miles and an eyesore."

Roo's feeling about getting the most out of things was echoed by another girl just about her age in Mankato, Minnesota. Jean Schemmel has been a vice president in her local Explorer Scouts and active in many projects. She became interested as an early teenager in the possibility of turning things back for reuse.

For two years Jean wheedled, cajoled and persuaded her family and neighbors to use everything possible a second time.

She talked people into helping her take materials to centers that would put them back into circulation. Finally, when she was old enough to drive a car, she hauled truckloads of trash herself.

It was at that point that we heard of her: she was tendered a radio salute over a Minneapolis station. "The earth needs more people like Jean," said the naturalist, Bob Duerr, in a broadcast account of her exploits. "Young and old alike."

So, it's not merely a case of closing your eyes to the Throwaway Syndrome in hopes that all that trash will go away. There are plenty of people turning garbage into gold. It's an especially cheering sign that the youngsters, unhampered by tradition and the "we've always done it this way" mentality, refuse to take gloom at its long-faced value, but optimistically look toward a better day.

With all the effort made in its behalf, I could build a whole book around the subject of recycling. There—I've said it: *recycling*. I've steered away from the word thus far in this chapter, as to me it somehow smacks of federal handouts, proclamations by the mayor and all kinds of litter laws—important as such official action may be. Only when it gets down to *people* does recycling come into proper focus for me.

I'm apt to turn the page when I read the legal jargon outlining Vermont's state law requiring a minimum five-cent deposit on beverage cans and bottles, but I nod in sympathy when the small storekeepers in my neighborhood say the law is ruining their business. At the same time I suggest to them that they see how similar laws have been made to work in Oregon, where anti-litter legislation has been in effect for years, or in Saskatchewan, where practically no can or bottle travels an inch without a price on its head.

Oregon's campaign for returnable rubbish has done a great job on roadsides over the whole state. Here in Vermont, one State Highway District supervisor says his crews have only a tenth of the can-and-bottle trash they had before the two-way container law went into effect. "People just don't toss 'em out any more," he said. "Or if they do, some hiker or bicycle rider with a saddlebag—or even somebody in a passing car—stops and gets 'em before we do."

Another Vermonter put it this way: "Who tosses away an empty six-pack these days? There goes thirty cents, right out the window."

As a final thought, I'd like to mention an Illinois man about whom I read in *Big Farmer* magazine. He reminds me of early days on my father's farm in Connecticut. One of the time-honored ways to dispose of animal manure is to spread it out on the fields. This is fine for the crops, but it has a startling effect on that pristine air, especially if the wind is right.

Such is not the case at the farm of Arnold N. May of Richmond, Illinois, however. He has found that when pig and cattle manure is mixed with urban sewage wastes, a biochemical reaction takes place that makes the resulting concoction nearly odorless. Spread on the soil by tank trucks, the triple-threat topdressing has more than doubled May's crop production.

The three ingredients are relatively easy to come by in Richmond. May feeds five hundred cattle and two thousand hogs. The city of Richmond, grateful for the chance to dispose of its waste so readily, pays him to get rid of it. He dumps it into a steel-reinforced receiving pit, twelve feet deep and the size of a swimming pool. "Then, by carefully mixing hog and cattle waste with city waste in the right proportion, and aerating and agitating the results, the odor is reduced by approximately eighty percent," he wrote me.

Some townspeople question that eighty percent figure, however. "I have had a great amount of resentment on the part of my neighbors and the public in the area," he continued in his letter. "They are imagining smells. They have complained to the Environmental Protection Agency and other government and health agencies. They are afraid that animals or dogs running anywhere in the fields might somehow contaminate or get the whole area sick. People refuse to look beyond pushing the plunger on a toilet; they feel, 'Whoops, I'm glad it's gone.'

"There has to be a final disposal method. Putting the material back into the soil enriches the soil, helps bring up the water table, and certainly conserves a very vital asset. It is worth many hundreds of millions of dollars when considered on a national basis. It certainly is much better than putting it into the water or using precious energy to burn it."

Big Farmer magazine pointed out that the fertilizer nutrients in that sludge have helped raise corn production on poor farmland from forty bushels per acre to over a hundred.

May is obviously doing something right.

CHAPTER SEVEN

Gullies Too Grim
for a Goat

NOT ALWAYS DO the self-styled improvement squads labor in limbo. Search the daily newspaper and you can usually find an account of someone's efforts to brighten a tiny corner of a gloomy world. Too often, such tales are elbowed aside by scare stories or are relegated to an inside page, but they are there if you search. Indeed, there's an encouraging trend to temper the bad with the good over the morning coffee—sometimes even on the front page.

Tanya Furman of Burton, Ohio, is such front-page news. We learned of her from the McCulloughs, whom you met in an earlier chapter. Tanya reached her thirteenth birthday a few months before I sat down to write these words. Yet so effective has her life been thus far that she has netted herself not only the satisfaction of a good job done, but a thousand-dollar prize as well.

It seems that when she was five, Tanya had a pet goat. She and Frisky went for walks around their property on the outskirts of town, exploring the woods, brushland and roads. One gully separating the Furmans' land from Snow Road was a favorite of the goat. Not only did it appeal to his mountain-climbing instincts, but it was liberally sprinkled with delicious-looking tin cans, broken glass and other assorted goat edibles.

Tanya, however, took a less jubilant view. There was so much trash in that gully that it was hazardous, even for a goat. So the youngster embarked on her own reclamation project.

"My mother, father, sister and I went along this gully for about a quarter mile and collected all the trash," she recalled in a letter to me. "There were mattresses, parts of cars, and televisions along with glass and beer cans. Every year since then, twice a year, we collect all the rubbish for what is now a half mile on each side of the road."

Tanya and her family also watched in dismay as the Ohio Bell and Illuminating Company cut a strip of roadside trees to free the telephone wires. Tanya kept after her father to complain to Ohio Bell. So effective was her prodding—and his protest—that the company agreed to replace the trees with a "living fence" of multiflora rose. The resulting hedge is now alive with wild birds and mammals.

Recently there was a car accident along the road; the dense mat of rose bushes cushioned the car's crash and prevented it from careening into the gully. Tongue in cheek, perhaps, the Furmans hastily persuaded the town trustees to put up a No Dumping sign along their stretch of road.

The National Wildlife Federation, through a contest in its youth publication, *Ranger Rick's Nature Magazine*, learned of Tanya and her efforts. So impressed was Ranger Rick, the knowledgeable raccoon who ostensibly edits the magazine, that he persuaded the Federation to award Tanya the first prize of a thousand-dollar scholarship.

She couldn't collect it right away, however. The scholarship was granted when she was only ten years old. She can claim it upon graduation from high school and acceptance by an accredited college or university. Meantime, Tanya continues her winning ways. While keeping that gully from backsliding she has netted a couple of second prizes, and a third and a fourth from Ranger Rick.

No more Ranger Rick prizes for her, however. Now that she's thirteen, the magazine says, she is too old.

A thousand miles southwest of Tanya's profitable hedge-and-gully lives another *Ranger Rick* winner. Bill Menzie earned his thousand dollars on an oil well. And he did it without selling a drop of oil.

We had been guests of Sandy and Bob Dark of Norman, Oklahoma. Sandy is an outdoor enthusiast and maintains an impressive file of clippings and publications at her curator's office in the Oklahoma City Zoo. Through her reading she learned of Bill Menzie, and asked him to her home to meet us.

The first glimpse I had of this remarkable young man was when a dusty automobile stopped in front of the Darks' house, and a tousled-haired boy stepped out. He walked hesitantly to the front door. "I'm Bill Menzie," he said, when we opened the door in response to his knock. And thus began one of the most delightful and rewarding days of our entire trip.

Bill introduced us to his parents, Donald and Jane Menzie, as we piled into the car. Then we headed out to see that thousand-dollar oil pit.

It wasn't long before I realized why the Menzies' car was dusty. Don Menzie is a professor of petroleum engineering at the University of Oklahoma in Norman, and spends long hours in the field. Today, however, the field trip was largely over improved roads—all except for the last jouncy quarter-mile along a wagon path through the Menzies' land to "Bill's acres," as Jane called them.

Our destination was the site of an old oil well, long since abandoned. Old drilling areas are usually wastelands, but this one was worth all the dust we had eaten in getting to it. Instead of oil-stained and dying vegetation, a half-acre pond

Near Norman, Oklahoma, Bill Menzie and his father Donald inspect a newly-budded branch growing on land, formerly an oil-well waste area, that Bill, then ten, worked hard to reclaim.

sparkled in the March sunlight. Birds sang in the bushes at the water's edge. One bird flew away from a nest box as we approached. Green little plants covered the soil, and the swelling scarlet jewels of the redbuds gave promise of the abundance to come.

"I had read an article in *Ranger Rick* nearly two years ago," Bill said. "It was called 'Living Things' and told how living things sort of lean on each other, that none of them can be independent. I got to thinking of the old oil-well mud-pit on our property, and how it was just about as wasted as any land could be. If any living things could ever use it, someone would have to clean it up for them. Maybe that someone was supposed to be me."

Ten-year-old Bill presented the idea to his father: Could he try his hand at reclaiming the pit?

He was so eager that his father let him go ahead. The rest of the story is best told by Bill himself—in the words he used in applying for that Ranger Rick prize of a thousand dollars:

"How did I *use* this article? I developed a *Ranger Rick Refuge.* In the article I read that 'living things depend on one another.' I think this means that maybe some living things depend on me. In our area much land is being cleared for grassland for cattle and homesteads. There is less and less land with enough [vegetation] for wild animals. In our land there is a large, fenced in, abandoned oil well 'mud-pit' which had been broken to allow the chemicals to drain. There were tracks of Ranger Rick's cousins, deer, opossum, quail and coyote around the pit, so we knew that the water was now all right for the animals to drink.

"East of the mud-pit is a small spring. Unfortunately the mud-pit and the spring both went dry during the summer and stayed dry until spring. I decided that the animals and birds here needed me to get them water and to improve the environment which the article said we all share. My first step in making my Ranger Rick Refuge was to close the hole in the dam of the mud-pit. I could not do this myself. My father arranged to have a bulldozer close the large hole.

"After the hole was closed I fixed up the fence so the cows would not get in. Mr. Jesse Murrell of the Federal Soil and Water Conservation Department came out and showed me how to stop the erosion. I planted rye grass first, then bermuda grass to hold the soil.

"A wildlife ranger from the Oklahoma Department of Wildlife Conservation came to help me plan how to make my acreage into a better 'habitat plot.' I took my January birthday money and bought $12.00 of plantings from the State Forestry Department."

Bill Menzie's letter goes on to tell how he dug overcrowded plants from nearby areas to put in the twenty-acre refuge. He set out hundreds of plants for food and cover: sunflowers for quail and cardinals, and fruit and nut trees for other birds and animals. He even grew small plants in pots on his windowsill for transplanting to the refuge.

Catfish were scheduled to go into the pond when the water cleared, and Bill brought in a hive of bees to pollinate the flowers and trees. He built bird houses and put them on fence posts. He filled eroded gullies on the area with old Christmas trees, gathered from the neighborhood with the aid of the family truck. The Christmas trees not only stopped further erosion, but served as shelters for wildlife. Their branches, with bits of tinsel still fluttering here and there, caught wind-blown seeds and sheltered them from the weather as they sprouted. The area, once desolate, now abounds in rabbits, mice, quail, opossums and other animals.

It was a revelation to contrast this lovingly tended tract with its surroundings. However, Bill disclosed something that warmed my heart even further. "I wanted to get more people interested in what they could do for living things," he said. "I didn't just want to keep it all to myself. So I enrolled my land in a program called 'Acres for Wildlife.' It's sponsored by the

Oklahoma Department of Wildlife Conservation."

The refuge was the first of its kind in the state. A Wildlife Department photographer took pictures for publicity all over Oklahoma. Bill took pictures, too: "before" and "after" shots of his Ranger Rick Refuge. He sent them along with his written contest entry, although pictures were not required.

The contest committee, perhaps overwhelmed with all the evidence, needed only routine proof of his eligibility. "Please express our delight to Bill for his fine writing," said the letter from the National Wildlife Federation on January 12, 1972. "A savings account in the amount of $1,000 will be opened in trust for Bill Menzie. . . . This college scholarship will be paid to you upon our notification that Bill has graduated from high school and has been accepted in college."

The real gain, of course, was far more than that thousand dollars. It will never be known what the impact of Bill's publicity pictures may be. Those twenty acres—now expanded to thirty-five of the family's 160-acre plot—have increased in value enormously. Bill has learned much about wildlife and its needs, as he abundantly demonstrated in the full morning we spent on the Ranger Rick Refuge, looking at plants and animals and rejuvenated land from the refreshing viewpoint of a fourteen-year-old.

Doubtless you have already suspected that this will not be the end of recognition for Bill Menzie and his oil well that produces no oil. Other accolades Bill has received to date include a certificate from the Oklahoma Department of Wildlife Conservation designating him an official "Outdoor Oklahoma Cover Agent," plus a letter from I. H. (Mutt) Standefer, the Department's director, congratulating him as co-winner of the Oklahoma Youth Conservationist Award. And, several months after we regretfully left the Sooner State, a letter from Sandy Dark told us that Bill was still going. To the growing list of his titles he has added that of Eagle Scout.

Sandy's letter, by the way, enclosed a portion of the Sunday section of the *Tulsa World*. It told of a ten-acre plot near Boynton, in eastern Oklahoma, where Future Farmers of America students worked with the Soil Conservation Service to rescue the desolate land around another extinct oil well.

The well, drilled before the turn of the century, had flowed with the salt water that often accompanies the precious black fluid. When it was abandoned, the well was plugged to prevent salt spillage, but the plug leaked and briny water flowed out over the ground. Vegetation died in its path, leaving the land open to erosion and gullies—and providing perfect channels for the salt to travel farther.

John Worthy, of the Okmulgee County Soil Conservation District, inspected the land with owner David Billings. Together they carried out the strategy—with plenty of willing help from FFA students of nearby Morris. They sealed off the well and smoothed crevices in the tired old land with a disc plow. A mulch of hay was put down, followed by salt-resistant grasses. Then the students planted hundreds of shrubs that would bind the soil while providing food and cover for wildlife: cedar, multiflora rose, mulberry, autumn olive.

Their efforts bore gratifying fruit. Fenced against livestock, the land now supports wild mammals and birds of many kinds. Indeed, the fortunes of the field boomed from the first. John Worthy told Gus McCaslin, author of that article in the *Tulsa Sunday World*, that they got results that were almost too good with the first thirteen hundred trees. "The rabbits ate them," he said, simply.

Such unqualified acceptance by wildlife could be a bit startling. But of course that's the whole point: the two basic wildlife needs are food and shelter. Sometimes the infant food plants need protection. Otherwise their potential users mow them down before roots and shoots get established.

Occasionally the soil itself is hostile to man's good intentions.

Dr. Charles Riley, biology professor at Kent State University in Ohio, found this to be the case in his efforts to hide the scars on some 150 acres of barren strip-mined land. The non-productive "overburden" of soil had been removed to expose a seam of coal several feet below the surface. One of the problems of such strip-mining is that the overturned land (often called "spoil") is toxic to many kinds of plants.

"You just cannot come in and scatter grass seed on strip-mined land," Dr. Riley told us as he spread a large map of the area on his kitchen table. "The spoilbanks—piles of discarded soil—left by the 'surface dig' are rank with soluble salts, sulfides and unmined coal. Runoff and ground water in puddles and ponds, after contact with these spoils, becomes highly acid."

He pointed out a little stream and three ponds on the map. "But as the vegetation slowly takes over," he said, "a change occurs on the barren land. Erosion can no longer expose fresh materials to leaching by the rain, and these watercourses become less acid. Certain trees, such as black locust, red pine and red oak, can do quite well. Sweet clover, lespedeza, and timothy will take hold after the land has had a chance to rest."

Riley began his studies in land reclamation as a graduate student at Ohio State University in 1946. He became so interested in the fate of strip-mined land that he bought his own "Riley's area" in 1948. Since then, almost without let-up, he has studied, probed, live-trapped animals and birds, taken hundreds of samples of soil and water to determine their *pH* (acid/alkaline balance). "In short," he said, "I've tried to keep my finger on the pulse for nearly thirty years."

In the process he has made some interesting observations. They carry a clear ray of hope for the future of strip-mined lands.

"Plant the right shrubs and trees," Riley said, "and you may eventually produce more plants and wildlife on this supposedly 'plundered' land than you can often find on nearby unmined land—or even on a good farm. The ponds will produce bass, bluegills, catfish, muskrats, frogs and waterfowl. We've studied over a hundred separate plots of land on all kinds of areas, planted more than seventy thousand trees, and live-trapped animals on reclaimed study areas totalling a thousand acres.

"Take the rabbit, for instance. Hunters and hikers and wildlife people all seem to like the cottontail. In a two-year live-trapping project, we figured out that there were 425 rabbits per thousand acres of reclaimed strip-mined land. This compared with 379 rabbits on an equal area of abandoned farmland, 75 on agricultural farmland, and only 50 on forest land. Reclaimed coal strip-land provides food, cover and water. That's just what most living creatures need.

"People look just at that big first step," Riley said. "But given time—and a little help in erosion control, pond establishment and planting of vegetation—you may actually have a good thing going in strip-land."

Strip-mined land has, indeed, been a "good thing" for Riley. After he got his master's degree he went on to study for the doctorate on his 140-acre laboratory. He bought a hundred more strip-mined acres in 1970; these are now growing a cash crop of Christmas trees. Today, in addition to being a consultant for the Ohio Reclamation Association, composed of companies engaged in the Ohio strip-mining industry, Riley is chairman of the Department of Biology at Kent State University. He has demonstrated, not only that mined land can be put to productive use, but also that, as he puts it, "the outdoorsman's future looks bright: successful reclamation of strip-lands for wildlife is no longer an idealist's dream. It has become a reality."

Nor is Dr. Riley's opinion merely that of a man who lives in a region where strip-mining is so important economically that to condemn it would be senseless. On his suggestion, Peg and I took a drive through the Ohio countryside toward the town of Cadiz, seventy miles to the south, to see for ourselves.

We drove past spoil-banks, yes—disheartening long stretches of them. And we saw the great draglines and power shovels at work. But we also saw rolling, manmade hills covered with vegetation; little marshes with cattails, reeds and rushes; we photographed expanses of grass and patches of new-growing shrubbery; a herd of curious Hereford cattle followed me as I sneaked up, camera in hand, on a mocking-bird swaying in a sapling—all this on reclaimed strip-mined land.

Just outside Cadiz we turned down a little drive and through an archway. The lettering on the archway told us we were entering Sallie Buffalo Park. Slowly, enjoying every inch of the way, we drove past picnic tables, playgrounds, winterized shelters, a little lake with its beaches. Although it was still January, several camping trailers waited patiently on their pads for the return of their owners.

Strip-mined land, too. And reclaimed a whole generation ago—long before the current push to save the soil got started. But there it is—one potential wasteland that is now enjoyed by many. The Hanna Coal Company, responsible for this pleasant little park—as it is for those reclaimed acres with their beef cattle and wildlife marshes—probably takes a grim satisfaction in the thought that the average person scarcely notices such areas—they fit too well into the scenery. Which, of course, is the whole point.

Another revelation took place when we went to visit Big Muskie. Big Muskie is the world's largest dragline. Owned and operated by the Ohio Power Company, the machine is used to remove the topsoil from above buried coal seams. Big Muskie swings a great flat bucket out at the end of two huge booms, drops the bucket and drags it back, scooping up as much as 220 cubic yards of earth with each "bite." Translated into terms more readily understood, 220 cubic yards is, roughly, the amount of space taken up by twelve full-sized automobiles.

We had been invited to be the guests of Ohio Power, and to meet Charles Keffler, Public Relations director. We did not approach the meeting without skepticism: after all, here was a conservationist-writer about to invade the enemy camp. They would, of course, show us only the best side. Nevertheless, we saw what we saw, and it was more than encouraging. If the mining companies' devastation of the land is on a large scale, so are their efforts to reclaim it.

As we approached the field office some twenty miles southeast of Zanesville, we could see the twin booms and pulleys of Big Muskie appearing and disappearing as it worked beyond a ridge five miles away. The booms were pointed right in our direction. How long, we wondered, would it take that behemoth and its attendant smaller brothers to dig their way to the peaceful Ohio countryside along our road?

The question was in my mind as we pulled up to the field office. There we met Mr. Keffler, who introduced us to Walter Smith. Mr. Smith, it seems, is a forester, one of two employed by the company. He asked us if we had driven down from Philo, where we had telephoned him the day before. When we nodded, Smith spoke up. "Then you must have driven past that land we finished grading the year before last."

It developed that Ohio Power's stripping machines had already come and gone along the road we had admired earlier that day. Behind them, bulldozers and graders had smoothed the earth. The two foresters—plus four agronomists, or soil specialists—had analyzed that earth, determined the best natural use for the land, and had planted grasses, shrubs, wildlife foods.

I asked Walter Smith about the size of Ohio Power's reclamation program. The program, I learned, is large, just like Big

Muskie. It is evidently more than a token effort to hide the effects of strip-mining. Over thirty million trees have been set out since the company's operations began in 1943. The thirty thousand-acre Ohio Recreation Lands in southeast Ohio, leased to the state by Ohio Power, provide camping, fishing, canoeing and nature study under replanted trees that are nearly thirty years old.

We spent much of the day with Charles Keffler and Walter Smith. We toured strip-mined areas, new and old, and watched Big Muskie at its never-ending task of setting aside as much as seventy-five vertical feet of earth lying above that much-sought seam of coal.

It is chilling to witness that great scoop as it lifts three hundred tons of payload and deposits it the length of a football field away, all in one smooth swing. The rumble of that 240-ton bucket, the growl of bulldozers and smaller shovels, can obviously never replace the song of the larks, the whisper of grass, the hidden sounds of mice, the scream of a hawk overhead. Yet such is the power of the earth to rebound that, once strip-mining has passed on, those larks and mice and hawks can return. By smoothing the soil and planting it, and otherwise giving nature a needed hand, we can help speed the day of their return by years—even centuries.

Months after our visit to Ohio, Mrs. Janet Mullins asked me about the coal-mining operations we had seen on our trip. She and her class in Orwell, Vermont, were studying the use of our natural resources. They agreed that many of our country's woes come from man's thirst for more and more comforts and luxuries, more than a few of them, it seemed, dependent on electricity generated by strip-mined coal. Janet got her students to wondering what they could do about it. But when she asked them which they'd give up first—radio, television, record player or home heat—they were at a loss for an answer. Suddenly they realized who were the *they* who wanted all those extras.

One child, however, gravely pondered the question and came up with his own fifth-grade solution. If it would help at all, he assured her, he'd give up his electric toothbrush.

We saw on our trip other ways man has tried to restore lands, rivers and lakes he has spoiled. The once "dead" Lake Erie shows encouraging signs of supporting a thriving fishery again: you can get a delicious fish dinner, courtesy of Lake Erie, at a number of restaurants near its shores. The Naugatuck River, a mile from my boyhood home, was once a fetid open sewer that flowed through western Connecticut. It was "reclaimed" after flood waters of a hurricane in the mid-1950's scoured the channel clean from the Massachusetts border to Long Island Sound. When the waters subsided, a number of drainpipes from homes, factories and stores bristled out from the river's banks, helping to embarrass whole towns into treating the ailing stream with more respect.

Before the hurricane not even seagulls, which have digestions like a trashmasher and will eat anything, would forage more than a mile or so up the river. Now the gulls are found many miles upstream. There are fish in the river, too: just minnows and killifish, it is true, but fish, nevertheless. Vegetation grows on the banks where once there was just a blue, slimy strip of no-man's-land along the river's edge. All because of a disastrous hurricane that shook people up and made them work together.

Often that co-operation is closer at hand than people may think. At a busy street intersection in Madison, Wisconsin, some old houses had been demolished, leaving a half-acre strewn with the rubbish of bricks and lumber. Plans were to bulldoze the rubble away and pave the area for a parking lot. Such a plan, it seemed, was in keeping with the general character of the area: tall buildings, a high-rise University of Wisconsin dormitory, another parking lot across the street.

However, there was one other building near that old lot, a structure known as Zoe Bayliss Co-Op—a women's co-operative dormitory. Sue Wiesner, at Zoe Bayliss, learned of the projected fate of the land and wondered if some better use might be made of that street corner. Among all these modern marvels there ought to be some place to relax. Possibly the struggling weeds and forlorn grass clumps on that land were trying to tell her something.

Sue talked with other dormitory residents. Was a parking lot really what that street corner had always needed? How about a peaceful little mini-park instead, for instance?

Other Zoe Bayliss residents agreed with her. Together they mounted an effort not merely to oppose the parking lot, but to substitute a plan of their own for an alternate use.

Their arguments were so persuasive that the Campus Planning Committee reversed its earlier decision—unanimously. The students could have their park, provided their initial enthusiasm held up. If the park did not meet with the Committee's esthetic standards on annual review, in would come the asphalt.

One hurdle passed.

But what kind of a park would it be? Suggestions were tossed around; finally it was decided to have an area that would be of the most benefit to both people and plants. The idea was to have a "microarboretum" of native Wisconsin flora. Then students could see actual living specimens at first hand, while visitors would be able to take a relaxing stroll—and learn a little Wisconsin natural history if they were so inclined.

Students of landscape design submitted plans for reclaiming the tiny scrap of Wisconsin scenery. Jodi Geiger, a graduate student in Landscape Architecture, developed the general layout. When the time came for cleanup, spreading topsoil and planting, the enthusiasm of those original girls caught up some two hundred students and friends who turned out for the job.

Now named Walden Park, the half-acre jewel is passed by some thirty thousand automobiles a day. A number of plants have succumbed to the lethal exhaust fumes, but their replacement is a relatively simple matter. Passing drivers must be surprised to come upon this bit of greenery in all that cement and brick. So intriguing is the little park, however, that many stop and explore it. One Sunday the park was featured in the *New York Times*.

I got in touch with Darrel G. Morrison, Associate Professor of Landscape Architecture at Wisconsin, who wrote the *Times* article. "Neighbors have been co-operative," he told me. "Vandalism is almost non-existent. Zoe Bayliss residents provide pretty effective policing, since their rooms overlook the park, and they feel a sense of attachment to it.

"While there were large numbers of students involved," his letter continued, "there was a small dedicated core group from Zoe Bayliss who worked consistently to make the park a reality. One of these, Bev Spreeman, has since transferred into Landscape Architecture and will be designing similar places herself. The majority of really dedicated workers in the park have been women students, and I think it's not purely through chance. Maybe the nurturing instinct is stronger in women than in men, even when it's nurturing of the earth. Just a thought. Linda Robinson was the park's caretaker the first summer. She really deserves much credit for its success."

Well, there you have a few of them—from a little girl and her pet goat, looking beneath the garbage and seeing a tiny vegetated valley, to a young woman looking beyond the street rubble and seeing a refreshing little park. To neither of them —nor to the many others like them who are trying to give our world a second chance—would you have granted much hope of success. Obviously, they're not about to turn the world upside down.

Not at all. Somebody else has already done that. Over much of our country, in fact, the land has been overturned several times. The homesteader cut its forests, the farmer broke its sod. Some of the earth in strip-mining country has even been mined before—by early methods that cut into exposed banks or stripped a few feet of soil by pick and shovel. So, traumatic as Big Muskie may be, for instance, as it helps supply the coal for the generators powering fifty-five Ohio counties, its depredations are nothing new.

As Professor René Dubos points out in the December 1972 *Smithsonian* magazine, much of the landscape we cherish is the result of man's "humanizing of the earth"—fashioning his surroundings into gardens, farms, parks. The mosaic of Old World farmlands, the verdure of irrigated valleys, the patchwork-quilt aspect of my own Vermont, whose open lands alternate with forest—these and many more examples show that man does not always and forever despoil, plunder, obliterate. Sometimes—if we but look and consider—we may find he has treated the land with wisdom and respect.

CHAPTER EIGHT

Beautification
Is a Four-Letter Word

''YOU WRITERS!'' sputtered the woman at the boat dock, "you're all alike. All I seem to hear lately are 'shun' words. Like pollu*shun*, for instance. Or eroshun, or reclamashun. And now you ask me about beautificashun. Don't you have any *fun* words?"

Her outburst took me by surprise, but she had a point. This woman, renting out boats on California's Salton Sea, doubtless got an earful daily—spoken and unspoken—from people who looked at the considerable clutter around her place. But, much as there was room for improvement, improvement would scarcely occur as long as well-meaning guests merely shook an admonishing finger at her. Besides, she could argue, all she did was supply the boats. It was the customers who brought the trash. And when I arrived, I put my foot right in the middle of it. Literally.

"When you're busy like I am," she said, indicating the waiting flotilla tied at the dock, "*beautification* becomes a four-letter word."

She could tell I wasn't there for a pleasant morning on the water. But I couldn't let her have the last word—even if it was *beautification*. I decided to tell her about the Floating Forest.

Now it was her turn to be surprised. "A floating forest?"

"That's right. But not floating on one of your boats—and not here on the Salton Sea."

In answer to the woman's unspoken question, I gave her a brief sketch of this most unusual "beautificashun" program. It took place in the 1950's and 1960's on the Great Lakes. Not around the edge, or on an offshore island or two. On the Lakes themselves. In fact, right on a ship.

The originator of the project was J. P. Perkins, who started out as a deckhand on a cargo vessel and eventually became a captain. In 1957, on a trip back from Michigan to his home in Conneaut, Ohio, he brought four small tamarack trees aboard his boat. Plants are occasionally found in ship's cargo and the dense evergreen foliage of these trees attracted little attention among the crates and boxes lashed on deck. The trees were quickly found by passing birds, however. The birds gratefully sought shelter there on their long flight across the water.

Here I stopped talking to the woman, wondering why I was really telling this to her, anyway. But she was intrigued, so I rummaged around in my notes until I found a letter from Mr. Perkins. "I always have been interested in the outdoors and birds," he had written, "so I thought I might find it more helpful if I could just get birds in a tree and photograph them with my movie camera. The next year, 1958, I had white spruce trees aboard and shot several good fall sequences. In 1960 I had the biggest batch of trees aboard ever, and it was really too many to handle on most ships, as they would need moving when [the] ship took on or discharged cargo. That year I had 14 evergreens in bushel baskets. They came aboard all balled and burlaped. A friend of mine owned a tract of land and furnished the trees for me over the years. . . .

"At the end of the season I usually gave the trees to friends or else brought them home and planted them in our yard. I always tried to get trees or shrubs from three to eight feet high just to vary the grouping. On some ships there was enough space to have the trees between the cargo hatches and on others the baskets had to be moved. This last item usually limited the number of trees. . . .

"Over the years I had such trees as white spruce, black spruce, balsam fir, white cedar, hemlock, white birch, poplar, tamarack, red osier dogwood, willow, mountain ash and wild gooseberry. In the fall I had cut trees such as spruce and mountain ash and balsam. These had to be kept in buckets of water and specially braced or tied. . . .

"When I changed ships I just got new trees. I was always very careful in asking the crew to do much besides watering the trees, because of the union. Most volunteered and helped anyway, and many went on to become good birders in their own right."

Here I stopped reading, but the boat-dock lady motioned me to continue. So I read her the balance of the letter. Perkins related how, when he became captain of a Great Lakes freighter, he had a regular little forest on the upper deck. His ship must have been impressive, heaving into port looking as if a bit of the north woods had broken loose in a storm. He put out birdseed among his trees, too. Some birds, lured by the daily handouts, actually took up quarters in the waterborne woodland for a week or two. They rode along through all kinds of weather, day after day. When nesting time arrived, however, they'd seek a more stable nursery for their young on shore.

When I had finished, I put the letter back in its envelope. I was about to leave, but the woman stopped me. "Never heard anything like that before," she said. "What'd you say your name was?"

I told her; then asked her for hers. She gave me her name, "but just make sure you don't put it in your book."

As we turned to leave, she added one last comment. "By

the way," she said, "you can forget what I told you about beautification. But I just wish they'd find a less fancy word for it."

There are, of course, many other less fancy words. The Junior Garden Club of Millinocket, Maine, composed of sixth-graders, might employ the time-honored phrase "Show and Tell." The club made a movie showing some of the less charming spots in its area, and suggesting what could be done to make them more attractive.

Jim Garner, editor-owner of "The Paper," a feisty little weekly in Prescott, Arizona, might say something like "Scream and Yell" as a synonym for *beautification.* As I sat in his back office, he explained how, when a certain little triangle of land was left in Prescott due to relocation and improvement of a street, city officials contracted with an oil company to put up a gas station. Garner got word of it and, through his paper, plus publicity in the daily *Prescott Courier,* raised such a ruckus that red-faced officials and the oil company hastily withdrew. Now, aided by the efforts of such groups as the Yavapai Citizens Association, that tiny triangle is a beauty spot. Snow-covered when we saw it in March, it welcomes visitors to Prescott during the growing season with shrubs, annuals, a little lawn.

A few hundred miles to the northeast, in Grand Junction, Colorado, members of the local garden club talked about beautification in terms of working together. Peg and I sat and watched for an hour as Grand Junction Park Department employees set out shrubs and flowers in a little grassy park at First and Grand streets. The land, we learned, is owned by the State of Colorado, but maintained by the City of Grand Junction, with plants supplied by the Desert Vista Garden Club.

We reflected that, in less fortunate cases, this acre would long since have been submerged in trash, or would have borne

The deck and superstructure of Captain J. P. Perkins's Great Lakes freighter are among the unexpected sites to profit from being embellished with forest greenery—and the birds that the greenery attracts (here, a female bobolink). (PHOTO BY J. P. PERKINS)

a crop of billboards. In Grand Junction, however, it provides a delightful welcome to travelers, because state, city and private citizens have helped each other to help it.

The little park also keeps that touch with nature that is so important to city dwellers. "I'm an old farmer," Sam Dupper, who waters the parks at night, told me, "and I love to work. Especially work like this. It keeps me young."

Such a spirit is found all over town, where each of the five garden clubs sponsors a certain number of little parks. The clubs provide the necessary vegetation, while the Parks Department provides the labor. Even the Grand Junction Men's Club gets in on the act, the men doing some of the planting themselves.

One area of special concern to the Men's Club is the nearby race track. The members have taken it as their task to beautify the grounds with plantings of annuals. "George is real dedicated to keeping an eye on those plants," one of the ladies told me, "especially on race days."

Much farther east, in Iron Mountain, Michigan, we happened along just as a group of 4-H youngsters was setting out flowers along a roadside. This group, the Green Thumbs 4-H Club, would probably mention *family* in comments about improvement: just two families account for ten of the eleven kids in the group, and the two mothers, Mrs. Paul Gauthier and Mrs. Robert Mellon, are co-leaders.

The Mellons and Gauthiers—plus odd-man-in Kevin Baudhuin—were planting, watering and weeding several little plots along the busy highway. Aided by two former leaders, Frank and Mary Peterson, they laughed and chatted and scratched in the soil, oblivious to traffic just a few feet away.

I watched as the wind created by a passing tractor-trailer temporarily flattened two rows of newly planted petunias. It seemed impossible that tender plants could live in such turbulence, but Frank Peterson just smiled. "The plants love it," he said. "Keeps the bugs off."

Bugs or not, those little garden plots have done well. The Green Thumbs were given an award by a grateful city, and in 1972 the group received a special plaque from Keep Michigan Beautiful, Inc. Furthermore, there is one bonus that none of those 4-H members expected. "It's funny, but nobody tosses stuff out on the flowers," Mrs, Gauthier told me. "Maybe a gum wrapper or two, but that's all."

Co-operation would be the byword, too, for beautification projects in Scottsdale, Arizona. There our friend Olive Rix took us out to a stretch of greenbelt known as Indian Bend Wash. "From an eyesore a few years ago," Mrs. Rix said, "this dry riverbed has turned into a ribbon of beauty and utility for eighty thousand people. When it's through being built, you'll be able to golf, picnic, watch the birds, enjoy the trees, or just walk if you're so inclined."

Indian Bend Wash flows right through the heart of Scottsdale. It receives flood waters once every year or so. Because of its infrequent flooding, there has been much pressure to let Scottsdale's growing population spill down into the wash. The flood waters, it was argued, could be channeled into a concrete trough going through the middle of this new development.

The idea seemed workable enough. The Army Corps of Engineers was consulted. It presented a plan for "channelization" of the wash, with a great fifteen-million-dollar concrete barrier to guide those rare flood waters. The plan was lumped with other county-wide projects into a bond issue that went before the voters in 1966.

"The bond issue didn't pass," Olive told us. "Perhaps it was the hand of fate. Lots of people were lukewarm about the whole idea, anyway. They couldn't see spending all that money on such an unsightly structure—especially when it would sit around useless except for one or two days every couple of years."

As a result the city sought the advice of a planning consultant named John Erickson, who came up with an alternate suggestion. Today, largely as a result of the "Erickson Report," much of the Indian Bend Wash land has been planted and is carefully watered and tended. Instead of a hot, dry gully 180 feet wide and 25 feet deep, the "sluice" is a place of shrubs, flowers and grass that everyone can enjoy.

Those flood waters, by the way, may still roar down Indian Bend Wash on occasion. This, of course, is nothing new; flash floods have been going on for as long as the earth has existed. In Scottsdale, however, with the help of a little creative imagination, flood waters will be controlled and even saved, to be released slowly in that arid land. The U.S. Bureau of Reclamation was planning a water storage area near by, anyway. By altering its plans it could provide the holding capacity needed to contain much of the water.

Intrigued that the Scottsdale City Council had been able to turn a "thumbs down" vote into good for the whole community, I wrote Marc G. Stragier, the city's Public Works director. Co-operation, he indicated, was the key. "That god-awful concrete gulch," as one Arizona newspaper called it, was not wholeheartedly accepted by the people of Scottsdale, anyway—no matter how good it looked on the drawing board. "But the [new] plan is simple, well underway, fully funded, fully supported," wrote Stragier, in a draft of an article about the project. "We'll get it done. It stands as a developing example of creative engineering. It is an example of response to growing concern about the quality of life."

Creative engineering was the key, too, in the town of Barrington, New Jersey, just south of Philadelphia. With a little imagination and industry, Barrington was able to improve things around one of the most dismal areas to be found in any city: the edge of the railroad tracks. Peg and I nearly caused an accident when we hastily pulled the car over to inspect a cribwork of old railroad ties that had been piled up on either side of the grade crossing.

The cribwork had been laid up, log-cabin fashion, until it was about as high as a person. The resulting enclosure had been filled in with stones, gravel and topsoil. Shrubs, flowers and little evergreens were growing in that soil, with a mulch of wood chips and organic material on top.

On inquiring, we discovered that Thomas Lunn, a local attorney, decided he had looked long enough at the grimy railroad crossing. Something should be done. He asked his fellow members of the town council how they'd improve it. Out of the suggestions evolved the idea of the cribwork. Lunn, greatly liked in Barrington, soon talked a number of individuals, plus civic, women's and youth groups, into helping clean up the area and build the new structures. "Getting everybody interested has helped keep it going," said a storekeeper when I asked him how the town felt about this bit of face-lifting. "We're all sort of proud of it—especially when strangers, like yourself, take the time to notice it."

Creative engineering, in a way, was also responsible for the unusual appearance of a park in Lake View, Iowa. Creative engineering, plus unwillingness to cast the first stone.

Named the Black Hawk State Park, the area was, without doubt, the cleanest American campground we saw on our entire trip. Even some of the sparkling Canadian campgrounds would be hard put to match it.

The creative part, I must admit, gave me a secret feeling of satisfaction. It involved something I had long suspected to be true, but had never before seen in operation. The idea was simple, but it seemed to work: put out so many garbage barrels that the potential litterbug just *couldn't* miss. No matter which way he was tempted to toss his trash, there was a container waiting for him.

The second part, about casting the first stone, was told me

by Dean Hall, Park Officer, who acts as mother hen to that astonishing collection of trash cans, plus the thirty thousand visitors the park may have on a good weekend. His men work hard, and he's quick to give them credit. "They keep it cleaned up," Dean stated, "so the public keeps it cleaned up, too. Even a bottletop sticks right out when it's the only one around. Everybody hates to toss that first bit of garbage."

Black Hawk Park wasn't always this clean. Those picnic tables didn't always seem almost new, either. The old carved initials had to be puttied and painted over. Recreation areas within the park had to be swept, raked, neat-cropped. Rest rooms had their share of graffiti to be removed—they were not always as bright and airy as they are now. "But we were lucky," says Dean Hall. "We were able to look beneath the surface and see how nice it could be."

And I guess he said it all, right there: beautification comes from the ability to look beneath the surface. Once you've seen how nice it *could* be, the rest is only developing that vision. This is what is happening in Creemore, Ontario, for instance, where the Creemore Horticultural Society systematically brings beauty through landscaping to a tired street corner, a vacant lot, an abandoned cellar hole.

The vision has also come to reality at an ARCO gasoline station on the outskirts of Los Angeles, where carefully tended shrubbery, sturdy playground equipment, and a shaded service area with a modern Spanish theme have won national recognition—and our personal gratitude on a blistering day. Similar efforts are evident at other companies' gasoline stations, which compete for the annual Highway Awards.

Community betterment projects all over the country are helping each other see the possibilities of improvement: Iowa City's project GREEN, for instance, which involves many of that college town's residents in everything from tree-planting to the annual Garden Fair; or my own state Jaycees' vow to freshen up all the AMTRAK railway stations in Vermont.

Possibly my Lady of the Lake at the Salton Sea may run across this book and recognize herself, even though I didn't mention her name. I doubt if I'll ever get the chance to talk with her in person again. However, at last I have the better word she wished for her "four-letter word," *beautification*.

I would suggest another four-letter word:

The word is *Care*—tender, loving care.

CHAPTER NINE

"... Our Most Important Product"

BETTER BACK UP a bit, as my Vermont neighbors would say. From what's been said so far, it might seem as if all the effort to improve our weary world is by people working alone or in little groups: The Saturday Sweepers, perhaps, or the Community Clutter Campaign.

Certainly they deserve all the credit they can get when, like Bill Menzie in Oklahoma, they suddenly realize that "some things depend on me." But we should not forget another whole chunk of modern life—the many-headed giant known as Industry. More and more, especially in recent years, industry is accepting responsibility for those aspects of a healthy outdoors that depend on it.

Part of this new look in industry, of course, is a result of the clamor put up by practically everybody against the wasteful ways we have all enjoyed for so long. Stiffened government regulations have a lot to do with the new look, too; and no doubt many of industry's efforts to act with more consideration for our environment are motivated by the fact that such efforts make good public relations.

We may, therefore, be tempted to object, concerning industrial conservation projects, that their motives are not pure.

But we should remember that the fish in the rejuvenated stream, the tree that gains a footing on reclaimed land, care not how or why things got better. They just reap the benefits. If they could think and talk, doubtless their comment would be: "So what if it's all to improve the company's image? If this is what they mean by improved public relations, more power to it!"

We discovered evidence of the new look in industry all across the country. We found it in many kinds of enterprises, from home builders to soup makers. We even found a company—strange as it sounds—that actually washes lakes and ponds.

Let's take that last one first. In order to get the picture, you'll have to adopt a familiar domestic pose: standing at the sink with your hands in the dishpan. Or, if you're allergic to dishwater, let's say you're cleaning parts of an engine. There you are—only half done, but the liquid in the pan is too dirty to go any further.

What do you do? Simple. You pour out the old liquid and fill the pan with new.

Now magnify that dishpan a few million times and there's your pond. For our purposes, let's make it a tired, worn-out pond, liberally salted with old bottles and automobile tires. Obviously what it needs is a complete change. And this is where the Crisafulli Company comes in.

Crisafulli, of Glendive, Montana, makes pumps. Not ordinary pumps, however, such as you might find in the cellar, or even at most fire stations, but big pumps—able to suck a foot of water out of a pond the size of a football field in less than two hours. And that's just with the eight-inch hose. Put in a hose twice as big and you'll cut the time to a third.

Big as the pump may be in capacity, it's easily towed around like a two-wheeled farm trailer or an outsized wheelbarrow. Dunk the end of it in the pond and start the engine, or hitch it to the power-take-off of the tractor. When the water is gone, remove all the junk. Then let the pond fill up again. Or, if fish or other aquatic life would be ruined should the pond be pumped dry, just run your pump at partial speed to keep pace with incoming water. This, in effect, washes your pond and rinses it, just as you did with those dishes.

Wildlife men have long dreamed of changing the water in this way. Pumps have been used before—the idea is not new with Crisafulli. In fact, the Crisafulli pump was originally designed to handle a big irrigation job. Only secondarily did it prove to be good for pond projects.

The pump can be used in wintertime, too, to aerate oxygen-starved water. Sometimes, when ice is thick, fish will crowd around any opening in a desperate attempt to breathe. You can even catch them with your hands.

At ice-covered Lake Emily, in southeastern Wisconsin, the fish were in just such straits. So the Crisafulli Company, in a test of its new system, pumped the water uphill out of the lake and allowed it to swish back down. Bubbling and swirling as it re-entered the lake, it multiplied its oxygen content tenfold—and saved 260 acres of gasping fish.

The versatile pump has many other uses. It can clean up sludge, oil, even floating debris—as it does daily on the Willamette River in Portland, Oregon. And one version sounds like fun to operate: a maneuverable, self-propelled "Aqua Sweeper." It's a sort of waterborne vacuum cleaner. You steer it this way and that, scooping up the floating remains of somebody's picnic or oil spill as handily as if you were piloting a motorboat.

"You might say that we can burn our candle at either end," Fran Mertes, Crisafulli's technical director, told me. "Some places want to have the water taken away, while others don't have enough. We can help them both, sometimes with the same pump and two long hoses—one in and one out."

We got a chuckle out of another firm with another sort of

At a paper-manufacturing plant in Arkansas, John Carter points out the company's "liquor" processing pool, in which waste water is cleansed and prepared for dispersal.

two-headed candle. This is the Campbell Soup Plant in Paris, Texas. Campbell uses great quantities of water in a day's work. Effluent from the plant used to run out along a dry riverbed, creating mini-flood conditions at the time of release. The flooding compounded erosion in that arid land. Wondering if some better use couldn't be made of the water, Campbell engineers came up with a clever idea.

Put into operation, the plan involved terracing and grassing-over that riverbed to create a long, winding, grassy spillway. Instead of pouring water out on the spillway, the plant sprays it out, thus aerating it and giving bacteria a helpful boost in reducing wastes in the water. The spray, falling to earth, irrigates and enriches the soil, creating a luxury crop of grass, which is harvested and sold as fine hay. The sale returns about a sixth of the program's cost.

What made us smile was a report by The Sports Foundation. This Foundation is a non-profit membership organization concerned with national recreation and resources. From its Chicago headquarters it sponsors annual awards to industries that aid our soil, water and wildlife. In granting its Gold Medal Award to the Campbell plant in Texas, the Foundation told how cattle actually prefer this hay, grown on what I suppose could be called watered-down Campbell Soup.

Other industries, once spendthrift in their ways, have taken on the new look. Time was when paper mills, for instance, were built right astride a stream. Coming in clear and cool, part of the water was channeled through the plant, spewing out as a brown or black "liquor" that made the river look like last week's coffee and smell like last month's eggs. Add to this a daily helping of bark and other waste for good measure, and the stuff was nearly ready for bottling.

"It's a little different now," said John Carter, Environmental Control Specialist at the Crossett Lumber Company in Crossett, Arkansas. "We have our own water supply: Lake

Georgia-Pacific, named after our parent corporation. Water, to us, becomes an endless belt. We use it to carry all kinds of materials: logs, wood chips, chemicals, raw paper, waste matter. We filter it, screen it, heat it, cool it, speed it up, let it settle."

Mr. Carter dipped a finger into a nearby trough along which water raced on the way to its next job. As he held his hand up, a single drop glistened from a fingertip. "See that drop? Before it's through, that drop will have traveled twelve miles and been with us three weeks."

When its task is finished, the water, suitably clarified and relieved of its many burdens, is sent to a pond. There it is aerated by several large bubblers. Mr. Carter took us to the pond; to our surprise, as we walked along the dam, several ducks flew off the water. Sandpipers poked along the edge; songbirds swayed in the overhanging branches.

"And this is your waste water?" What I had meant to be a statement came out as a question.

He smiled. "This is our waste water. Nearly half a square mile of it."

And where does that water go after it leaves the pond? Down to the nearby Ouachita River. There, rich in oxygen, it has actually improved living conditions for fish. It has earned a Sports Foundation award for that Georgia-Pacific plant in Crossett, too.

On a trip to northern Maine, we were guests of the American Forest Institute, along with a group of outdoor writers and editors. We flew, rode and hiked over thousands of acres of lands of Great Northern and Scott Paper companies. We saw other evidence of the changes that have taken place in the timber industry.

One big difference is that great areas are no longer stripped of trees and left bare. In many places only mature trees are taken. In others, where clearcutting is practiced, the operation is done in small chunks of a few acres. Thus the trees left standing on either side send their seeds into the cleared area by wind, birds and squirrels. In this way the company, in its tree-harvesting, works with the normal processes of nature, instead of leaving the new forest to chance.

"In place of the old cut-and-get-out philosophy, the modern lumberman plans it so the land produces trees continuously," Lester Decoster, the Institute's New England Regional Manager, told us. "The seedling is as important as the mature tree."

Personally, I enjoy the sight of a great tree standing there, even if it does represent boards for houses, wood for the fire, pulp for the pages of this book. A newly clearcut area is a sorry sight. Branches and tree tops are strewn everywhere. Spruce and balsam needles shroud the ground, often mercifully covering those bereft stumps. Even the host of tiny seedlings, already poking up through the litter, seem wholly inadequate ever to cover this desolation.

But then, as Mr. Decoster reminded us that day in Maine, this is what the rest of the forest was once like, too. Under a system of clearcutting in little patches like this, the trees will come back.

And they do. To prove his point, Mr. Decoster took us to three different growth-areas. One had been clearcut two years ago, one six years, one sixteen.

On the two-year area we could still pick out the cut-down branches and tops. They were half hidden, however, as around and through them poked quick-growing plants. There were a few daisies and grasses, but much of the greenery was made of raspberries, dewberries, blackberries and wild rose. Mr. Decoster explained that these are often known as "nurse plants." He pulled away a raspberry to show beneath it a spruce seedling six inches high. "The nurse plants serve to shelter seedling trees in their first years. Birds and animals bring in the seeds of these nurse plants in their droppings.

They 'plant' them, complete with a little pat of fertilizer—all ready to grow."

These creatures were much in evidence. Trails of mice threaded the ground like roads on a map. Twigs, sharply nipped off for their buds, showed the typical slanting cut made by mice, rabbits and others of the buck-tooth set. Birds flitted through the low growth, searching for insects. In fact, there was far more wildlife here than in a dark, quiet virgin forest, with its shadows and its parklike forest floor.

The six-year forest plot had bushes as high as our heads. Some of the little spruce and fir trees were nearly as tall as the bushes. Now we saw evidence of larger animals: the frayed twigs typical of the feeding of the deer, which lacks a set of upper front teeth and must break its food off with lower teeth and tongue. We saw the tracks of a moose, too, and the droppings of a fox in the dust along the road. More slanting-cut twigs of rodents and rabbits, plus more birds, more insects.

Ten years later—the sixteen-year plot—the area was already a little evergreen woodland. Alders were pushing up beneath the spruces and firs but they'd soon give way. Maples, more persistent, were shouldering for the best light. The nurse plants, their task completed, were spindly and shaded. Some of the spruces, we estimated, were twelve feet high—they had grown nearly a foot a year once they had gotten started. There were still birds and mammals, but those insects had gone to sunnier spots. In less than two decades, the woods had returned.

Many Maine forests can reproduce themselves in this way after cutting, Mr. Decoster pointed out. Not all the forests are left to restore themselves, however. On millions of acres all over the country new little trees are planted shortly after the big ones are cut. Fire, disease and insects are vitally important to companies that trade in forest products. Control methods that these companies have worked out benefit everybody, not just the companies and their trees.

Later, after our Maine visit had ended and we were on the way home, I thought back on what Mr. Decoster had said. One of the biggest changes in the industry, I realized, was that we had made the trip at all. For generations, companies using our natural resources have gone their way—the public be damned. Doubtless there are many practices that still won't stand the light of day, but at least we now have some chance to poke and prowl and peer about. We can ask questions—on location, face-to-face. This, I believe, is a new and encouraging sign.

There are encouraging signs, too, at the other end of the lumber industry. In home-building, you can spot a number of changes from the post-World War II days, when trees and rocks were merely in the way of new construction. I remember one such early housing development: Peg and I were offered the inducement of "four little maple trees planted right on your lawn, Mr. Rood, so your new home is all landscaped"—while less than a block away a huge pile of twisted trunks and limbs proclaimed that the whole area had been forested just a few short weeks ago.

Of course there have always been those who have laid their building plans with care and respect for the land. Now, happily, their numbers are increasing. Some forms of cluster housing, for instance, arrange new-built homes with an eye to a little natural area that is allowed to go unscathed alongside all that construction. When the new residents move in, the wild area remains, untouched, as part of the new development, thus giving the plants and animals—and people—the elbow room they need.

Even the trailer park has softened its stark outlines. A site for such a park near my parents' home in Terryville, Connecticut, was abundantly blessed with trees and shrubs before the advent of its first mobile home. As every new unit was wheeled into place, the greenery was carefully tied out of the way—even dug up, set aside and replanted. Now, after several years, each occupant is scarcely aware of his neighbor a hundred feet away in the bushes. If it weren't for an escape route at the front of every mobile home so it can eventually be hauled away, the whole affair would be like a boat in a basement—put together with no thought as to the way out. As it is, this woodland trailer park has eased into the scenery with scarcely the snap of a twig. You have the feeling that it could be spirited away, if needed, just the same way.

The woodland inhabitants have taken this colony of humans and their glass-and-metal nests right in stride. Half a hundred dooryards and trash cans are regularly visited by opossums and raccoons, who act as a nocturnal cleanup crew. Now and then a fox pays a visit, while an occasional skunk, pottering peacefully along in its absentminded way, may amble myopically into a yard belonging to an alert but misinformed canine—thus providing several dozen residents of Sylvan Acres with a more authentically woodsy atmosphere than they bargained for.

On a smaller scale, take the example of Dale Cahill, a custom builder in Prescott, Arizona. His "workshop," as he calls it, is composed of steep slopes, great boulders, giant pines, high altitudes and that refreshing Arizona air.

I first became aware of Dale's maverick way of building when I noted a house with a tree in it. Not a potted palm or an indoor rubber plant, but a good-sized ponderosa pine, growing right up through the roof.

When I got back that evening to the home of friends with whom we were staying in Prescott, I remarked about the odd house we had seen. "Oh, that's one of Cahill's homes," Les Jaquith said. "He's got a lot more than that."

We arranged with Dale for a tour of some of his homes, and discovered that he did, indeed, have more than that. This work-roughened, weatherbeaten man put us in mind of a steamfitter, perhaps, or a lumberjack. But as he took us to visit one home after another, a new and fascinating person emerged. He spoke with quiet respect of rocks, trees and hills as other men speak of blooded horses or treasured hunting dogs.

"It seems to be the practice to scalp a chunk of land," Dale told us. "We don't feel that way. We like our houses to look as if they've been there a while right after they're done—as if they've been in that spot for fifty years. We want to build *in* a piece of property—not just *on* it."

And he does what he says. We visited the home of John Burke as an example of Dale's building. The site chosen was a nice spot for a rambling house—except for a clump of three trees right in the middle of the lot. "But they're nice trees," Dale said, stroking the bark of one, a foot-thick pine, "so we decided to arrange the house around them, as you see. Besides, the trees have their rights, too. They were here first."

The house is in a modified U-shape, with those trees serving as a warm, if somewhat startling, welcome to the visitor. "People love 'em," John Burke assured us. "At first we thought they'd be in the way, but now we realize they're something special."

Another home, in nearby Shalimar, was under construction at the time. "A large juniper just happens to be where we needed to have the driveway," Dale told us. "So people are going to have to go right and left around that tree. But it'll be fun, and it'll look great."

We saw other Cahill homes, too, that were built right into the land. One driveway was sandwiched between two huge boulders ("they'll be all right—unless the folks want a grand piano"), while another house cleverly used native rock in roof and walls so you had to look twice to find a house there at all. And the house with the pine through the roof, we learned, belonged to Mrs. Lillian Blyth, herself an ardent nature fan. She had asked Dale to build the tree portion as a combined porch-utility room. When it rains, moisture follows the trunk down through the floor into the ground.

Some of the branches grow right inside the room. "They get enough light through the windows to hang onto their needles," Mrs. Blyth said. "It's sort of like living in your own Christmas tree."

Many of Dale Cahill's painstaking efforts never show at all. If small trees are in a house area, he digs them out with a backhoe, sets them aside in a trench, and replaces them when he is through. If roots are exposed on the edge of a bank, he wraps the roots in moist burlap until the bank is backfilled later. "Or you take dynamite," he said. "Sometimes you have to use it. In blasting rock, the gases from dynamite are deadly to tree roots—especially pines. If a whole area is raised by the blast, gases go all through the soil. But if you flood each tree with a hose right after the blast you get rid of those gases."

One time Dale had to install a complete sewage system for a house before starting in to build it—septic tank, supply pipe, dry well and leach field. "Otherwise we'd have had to go around the house to put it in, and that would've meant trampling down a lot of bushes and moving some perfectly good rocks."

Since there are few builders and land developers as careful as Dale Cahill, a whole host of regulations—and regulatory agencies—have sprung up to try to keep them honest. Here in Vermont, for instance, we have our unique Act 250. This law was hammered out in Montpelier in 1969 by a startled legislature when it seemed that our tiny Green Mountain state was to be colonized by foreigners from "down country"—as anyplace outside Vermont is called. Great plans were unveiled for apartment complexes, condominiums, and even instant villages. The thought of housing all the resulting newcomers, and attracting more, threw local town fathers into a panic as they considered the strain on schools, sewers and security.

Now, thanks to Act 250, any development of over ten

acres or ten housing units goes under the scrutiny of a county planning commission and the state health department—as well as the authorities of the town involved. The proposed development—commercial or residential—must dovetail with a statewide survey of present and proposed uses and capacities of land. The survey is a guide set up so that factories, homes and other construction will locate where they'll fit with the least amount of upset to their neighbors, wild and otherwise.

"Act 250 is a regulatory statute which makes it mandatory for developments which are large enough to have regional and state impact to receive permits before being initiated," says Addison County state senator Arthur Gibb, who has worked tirelessly on the act since its beginning. "We have thus established at the state level control over large-scale development."

Senator Gibb points out that the act calls for the adoption of land capability and land-use plans by the Vermont Legislature "in order to give legal validity to the use of such regulatory power, and to give district environmental commissions further criteria on which to base their decisions. No other state to date has adopted similar land-use planning, and we are therefore breaking new ground and have no precedents to guide us."

Other states are keenly interested, however, as are the various Provinces of Vermont's giant neighbor to the north. Senator Gibb tells me that visitors, letters, requests for information come from all over America to determine how a counterpart of Act 250 might work in Alberta, say, or Georgia or Louisiana.

And how has it worked in Vermont? "Great—just great," he told me. "The act has done exactly what it set out to do: regulate, rather than eliminate, new building projects. It has done its job well."

When I asked him for figures on the act's performance, he told me that there were more than a thousand applications for large-scale construction permits in the first three years of operation under the new law. "The state regulatory board okayed all but about three dozen of them," he said, "provided they met certain conditions. But in applying for a permit in the first place, the prospective builder has to think things through. And such foresight generally makes sense, all around."

There's a good parallel, he points out, between the regulations imposed by Act 250 and the hassle surrounding the Alaska oil pipeline. When it became apparent that you couldn't just string a tube across the tundra, the line's proponents had to take a long second look. Now, Gibb says, although it's to be erected in spite of continuing bitter protest, the resulting pipeline will be the most sophisticated structure of its kind ever built—with precautions and safeguards it never would have had without the clamor set up by its foes.

Doubtless Vermont's fledgling Act 250 faces many unforseen troubles. Refinements to the land-use plan are still being introduced. There'll be requests for plenty of variances—as there are in Hawaii, for instance, where a similar but less sweeping land-use plan has been in effect for more than a decade. The needs of "second home" developments, commercial interests, and new industry will have to be heard. Yet, by meeting the act's requirements before getting that permit, each applicant improves his own position. Adequate sewage disposal, a dependable water supply, a more-than-passing nod in the direction of the good earth and its creatures, all must receive due consideration before that new subdivision or factory can get started.

Even in places with no state law bearing down on the land and its use, you can find further examples of industry's attempt to become a better neighbor. The Allison Lumber Company, of Bellamy, Alabama, leaves uncut greenbelts of woodland along its drainage ditches and creeks as avenues for opossum, raccoon, foxes and a host of other creatures—and, with a smile, puts up a sign saying Forest Under Construction on newly planted land.

There's also the United States Brewer's Association. Red-faced at all the unwanted publicity its members get along the roadsides, the Association has initiated the campaign to "Pitch In!" And speaking of brewers, the Miller Company recently presented about sixty acres of Tamarack Swamp to the town of Menomonee Falls, near Milwaukee. The company hopes to persuade other owners of the swamp, nearly two square miles in size, to do the same.

Yes, there's a new look to industry, all right. I've given just a few examples; you can find many more, if you look. Take, for instance, a great enterprise like Del Monte fruits, giving away thousands of National Parks Coloring Books. Or consider Jack and Betty Peters in my little Vermont town, giving away bags of food from their country store so that a local flock of icebound ducks will not starve.

Good public relations, to be sure. And, therefore, good business. But the kids with those coloring books learned something about our national parks.

The ducks got their dinner, too.

CHAPTER TEN

Backyards
and Bulldozers

YOU HAVE SEEN HIM in cartoons. He's been in the movies and on the TV evening news. He has been in newspapers and magazines, too. He's tall, short, old, young—standing there, arms folded, daring the bulldozer to come one inch further.

We saw him in person. His name is Willis Combs, and he lives on the island of Sanibel, Florida. Willis brought his bride to Sanibel in 1952—long before there was a bridge connection to the mainland near Ft. Myers. They arrived by boat, looked the area over and purchased a tiny strip of land. The land, a hundred feet wide and six hundred feet deep, ran straight back from the sands of the Gulf of Mexico, famous at Sanibel for sea shells.

Soon the Combses started settling in. Willis helped build a little cottage ("actually, three of us did it—the carpenter, the stone mason and me"), while Opal transformed the scrub palmettos and sand dunes into a tiny plant preserve. "We cherish every inch of our acre and a half," Opal told us. "It's been our life for more than twenty years. We loved it into being."

And they have, indeed, "loved it into being"—the Woodmere Preserve Arboretum, with its hundred-odd labeled plants, plus some three hundred more unlabeled that the Combses know by name. You'll find it, if you go there, at the terminus of Gulf Drive. The pavement ends at the Combses' property line.

Then came the bridge. Long, low, spanning five miles of those shallow waters from the mainland to Sanibel, it brought change to the island—great, sweeping changes, with parking lots and motels and condominiums where herons once roosted and alligators drifted through the swamps. Willis and Opal had joined to fight the bridge; progress, however, finally won out. "But we still hope it'll disappear," Willis said. "I've prayed for a good hurricane for ten years."

No hurricane did the job, however, and in 1970 Progress arrived at the end of Gulf Drive. Searching through old records, the authorities discovered a forgotten easement, or right-of-way, extending onward from Gulf Drive. If opened up, the easement would allow more property to be used for development. And—you guessed it—the easement led right through the Combses' Woodmere Preserve.

"I didn't know what was happening," Willis said. "All I knew was that I was out in the yard one day when I suddenly heard some bulldozer noise. When it got louder I realized it was coming our way."

He ran out to the end of the street. Three of his sea grape shrubs were down. The bulldozer had backed up to push them aside. "At this point I saw red. 'What do you think you're doing?' I yelled at the man. 'We're clearing this easement through here,' he yelled back at me.

" 'The hell you are!' I told him. 'You aren't going to run a bulldozer right through a natural history preserve!' I stood my ground, and he got off his machine and drove away in his truck. We never saw him again."

What about those easement rights? "Well, that was a year and a half ago. They took the bulldozer away, and they haven't been back yet. I guess they could see I meant business."

Time will tell, of course, if Willis Combs made his one-man zoning campaign really stick. But it's the fire and courage of such people that may yet save us from the ruin that, statistics say, is inevitable. In the meantime you'll continue to see Willis in the news and cartoons. You can read more about him, too, in *National Wildlife* for December, 1971.

Go up the Atlantic seaboard a thousand miles and you'll come to someone else the statistics couldn't have predicted: a concert violinist who likes weeds.

This improbable combination exists in the person of Mrs. Richard Collins, of Kensington, Maryland. Margot and her husband, Dick, are both violinists. From their house on Homewood Parkway they commute to Washington to play in the symphony orchestra.

Homewood Parkway is a quiet boulevard in a residential section of Kensington. Down the center runs a grassy strip about a hundred feet wide. The strip has a tiny valley, threaded by a little stream choked with weeds and brush. The Collins children, Rob, Joni and Liz, used to look for lions and tigers along that stream—although now that Rob and Joni are teenagers the ferocious beasts have dwindled to squirrels, perhaps, or the neighbor's cat.

Dick and Margot roam the grassy lane, too. Margot took us to a certain spot in that center strip where she could go to enjoy the shade of a weeping willow and compose herself for a long, grueling rehearsal. "I love these weeds and bushes," she said. "I hardly know any of their names but I love them all."

Her neighbors relax there, too, "sometimes listening to the birds and sometimes just walking. Occasionally we have a mosquito, but we really don't mind it."

Somebody, however, apparently *did* mind the mosquitoes.

Besides, there were bees in the flowers. Sometimes, too, the creek overran its banks, flooding the greenbelt. So in the summer of 1972, a plan was announced whereby the county (which maintained the road and periodically mowed the grass) would take care of the situation. The creek would henceforth flow through a culvert running lengthwise through the center strip. Over the culvert would be placed a sidewalk. The odorous, disease-producing growth would be removed, and in its place would be a fine walkway.

The residents of Homewood Parkway were crestfallen. Their private little acreage was about to disappear. The delightful brook would be forced to run underground. But they shrugged—this was the way things went these days. And who could fight the county?

So it went for several weeks. The time drew near to "enclose the open ditch from Drumm Avenue to and through Grant Avenue along Homewood Parkway," as the official project description read. Then one day, as Margot pushed through those weeds for perhaps the last time, "I asked myself whose 'ditch' was this, anyway? If we didn't want it covered over, why did we have to have it?"

So she decided to do something herself. "I didn't know more than half a dozen people on the whole street," she said, "and I was scared to death. I'm not the type to knock on doors, but someone had to do it. So I took around a piece of paper."

The paper was a petition. Not a fancy-phrased work of legal art, but the plain thoughts of Margot Collins and a couple of friends: "We feel that our creek, with its large willow trees growing from it, is a positive asset to our street, providing an attractive screen of foliage that adds to the property value.

"This creek is always free flowing and never stagnant, and to enclose it is totally unnecessary and would be a complete

In Lincoln, Vermont, townspeople joined forces to save a forty-acre hillside from becoming a housing development. The area is now a recreational common for the town, complete with ski trails and a rope-tow.

waste of the taxpayers' money, which could be used to better advantage elsewhere."

The residents of Homewood Parkway were surprised to see Margot. "A few of them recognized me as the woman across the way, but many thought I was selling something. A couple of them slammed the door in my face before I could even explain. Then I'd go away and come back later."

One or two of Margot's neighbors caught the spirit. They took petitions of their own, and filled in the gaps in Margot's. When they were finished, residents of all but five or six of Homewood Parkway's fifty homes were lined up with Margot. She had seventy-four signatures.

Hurriedly, she trotted her "piece of paper" to the Montgomery County Department of Public Works. And it was here that she won her seventy-fifth—and most important—acceptance.

"Well, I'll be darned," the county official told her when she showed him the petition. "You don't want it either. Here at Public Works we'd rather not cover that creek, anyway. We feel just as you do: the money can be better used elsewhere. We thought everybody wanted us to do it."

Elated, Margot went back with the good news. "Simple as that," she marveled to her family, scarce believing her own words. "All it took was to stand up for something. Just as simple as that."

Nor is that all. As we wandered along that greenbelt with the Collins family, people waved to us and tooted their horns as they went by. "I've made a lot of new friends," Margot said. "And so has everybody else. We've still got the bees and the skeeters and the 'ditch.' But we're all ahead of the game, because we've got a whole bunch of new neighbors."

Across the continent, in San Clemente, California, lives a dynamic counterpart of Margot Collins. We learned of her after a tour through the starkly beautiful scenery of Anza-Borrego

Desert State Park, just north of the Mexican border. We were surprised, as we drove through the park, to see motorcycles scrambling up a sandy cliff. There were more bikes at the base of the cliff, plus about two dozen cars.

Everybody seemed to be having a great time, but we were puzzled. Somehow we had never thought of racing bikes as normal denizens of state parks. When we stopped in Thermal to Visit Glenn Vargas, a mineralogist who teaches at the nearby College of the Desert, we mentioned those motorcycles.

"Oh, that must be one of Joe Read's trouble spots," he said.

"Joe Read?"

"Mrs. Henry T. Read. She's a member of the Desert Protective Council. You have already seen what a great place the Anza-Borrego Desert Park is, but it's really like a sieve. Within its boundaries are many private holdings, some big, some small. So it's really full of holes—more than a thousand of them—like that motorcycle track you saw. Josephine— 'Joe'—Read is trying to fill in those holes."

We learned that Mrs. Read is familiar with the location of many of these "inholdings," as they are called. Where possible, her Anza-Borrego Committee tries to persuade the owner of the land to turn it over to the Park as a gift or as a living memorial. When this cannot be done, the Committee makes an effort to purchase the land. Money for purchases comes through donations and through "Joe" Read's tireless efforts.

Thousands of acres have been accounted for, thus far. However, some sixty thousand-plus acres are still "outside"— but within—the Park. "It takes fifteen generations, or five hundred years, for nature to restore a desert area once the vegetation has been taken from it," says a brochure about this fragile region. "With our shrinking wilderness this might as well be forever."

We did not get the chance to meet Mrs. Read; she was off on the trail of a parcel of land—perhaps to find an alternate hill for the bikes to climb. The result that this lively friend of the often friendless desert is working for is the opposite of Margot Collins's, so to speak: Mrs. Read is trying to persuade private interest to yield to the public good. Both ladies, in a way, are like Willis Combs—confronting that bulldozer.

A person standing in front of a bulldozer is an interesting sight, but even more surprising is that of a bird holding its ground in front of a military tank—and winning. The bird in question here is the California least tern, a threatened species within an ace of being wiped off the face of the earth. The tank—or tanks, for there are many of them—are based at the gigantic Camp Pendleton Marine Corps Base, California.

The California least tern nests primarily in disturbed sand. Plain, flat sand will not do; neither will grassy dunes. Where the sand is mussed, however, whether from children playing or from tanks on maneuvers, the graceful bird lays its eggs. Speckled and tan in color, the eggs match the sand and are almost impossible to see.

The parent birds are quick to defend the nest and young. They dive at any intruder, no matter how big and forbidding—even if it's a fullgrown tank.

One spring day a few years ago, the commanders and men of a tank unit noticed the terns circling and fluttering around them, and it wasn't long before someone discovered eggs and baby birds, crushed flat.

A quick check determined the species of the sparrow-sized bird with the forked tail. Further checking disclosed that the public beaches were so crowded with people and pets that the birds could not nest there. One of the tern's last desperate stands was being made here on the Pendleton shores—right where the Marines practiced amphibious landings.

Hastily, the Marines retreated. They left the beachhead in full command of the terns. After that, the tanks practiced their maneuvers elsewhere while, armed with binoculars and spotting scopes, their less mechanized buddies went back to reconnoiter.

The scouting party was disappointed. Hardly a nest did they see. There were only a few terns coursing over the waves, hovering, as is their custom, and dropping into the water after fish. Seldom did they bring the fish inland to a brooding mate or waiting young.

Had those tank treads put an end to that rookery of these dainty cousins of the seagulls? These California least terns—unique in American history in forcing the Marines to back down—had they been vanquished after all? Peg, who is an ex-Marine from World War II, had read about the puzzle in one of her newsletters. We both were curious to know the outcome.

We were met at Base Headquarters by Major George R. Schipper, Pendleton's Public Relations Officer. When we inquired about the terns, he smiled. "They are now alive and well, thanks. At last count there were about five hundred of them. That's a big jump from the thirty-eight adults and ten young we saw when they were at their lowest some years ago."

The next question, of course, was how the Marines had ever managed to swing the pendulum the other way. "Nothing to it. When we kept the tanks off the sand completely, the area didn't seem to be scuffed up enough for the terns to nest. So now we let the tanks in before breeding time to roughen things up a bit. The terns love to nest in the track marks. Then the tanks stay out until nesting is over."

Throwing life preservers to foundering sea birds is not the only feather in Pendleton's camouflaged helmet, however. Major Schipper put us in touch with William D. Taylor,

Natural Resources Director for the base. "There was the award, too," Taylor told us. "Made us feel pretty good, with two hundred military posts competing."

The honor, conferred by Defense Secretary Melvin Laird in 1972, was the Secretary of Defense National Resources Conservation Award. It came about partly as the result of other top-secret operations: spying on those terns at night with "starlight" sniper scopes; snooping on wandering deer who had been "bugged" with tiny radio transmitters; and launching an assault on hundreds of acres of clogged wetlands to help those lands revert to good marsh, swamp and lake again. Instead of planting mines, the Marines sowed seeds of edible plants—"liberating" ducks and shore birds in this case instead of some war-torn beachhead.

One Marine project that tickled me was a new use for explosives—what military men sometimes call "cratering charges" of TNT. Placing these at intervals, with smaller charges between, like a gigantic string of beads, they detonated the whole affair, creating a continuous chain of potholes. The scanty rain, aided by ground seepage, filled these holes, thus providing watering places.

Doves, quail, rabbits and other animals increased because of this water, which was "formerly lost by rapid infiltration and evapotranspiration," to quote the official report—which in plain language means the water had leaked out and dried up.

Camp Pendleton's shoreline is the only major remaining strip of natural beach between San Diego and Los Angeles. The beach is visited by outdoorsmen and as many as six thousand Girl- and Boy Scouts each year. In riding over the marshes and fields and dunes we were reminded of another primitive beach area we had seen—quite different, but also rescued right in the path of rumbling machinery.

This area, nearly two thousand miles from Camp Pendleton, is known as the Ridges Sanctuary. It is at Bailey's Harbor, in Door County, Wisconsin, near the tip of the peninsula that stretches northeast into Lake Michigan from the city of Green Bay.

Generations ago, range light installations on the peninsula were used for navigation. After they fell into disuse, the federal government turned the land over to the county in 1936 for use as a park. Almost at once, a campaign was mounted to convert the ridges into a campground.

In other places, perhaps, such a campground might have been a welcome alternative to some fancy building project. But the ridges are unique. Paralleling the shore of Lake Michigan, they are the remains of former beaches. Piled with debris, the old beaches gave lodging to plants which grew to form a natural sand fence. Wind piled the sand along this "fence" and another ridge was formed.

There are about a dozen of these ridges at Bailey's Harbor, some as big as the raised bed of a highway. Between each ridge and the next is a ditch or slough. The stable condition of the water in the slough, plus the sandy bottom, may make for acid conditions, which favor the growth of many unusual bog plants. Pitcher plants lift their cupped leaves to trap and digest unwary insects, and more than two dozen species of native orchids make the area fascinating to wildflower enthusiasts. In other places limestone pokes out, creating an alkaline condition. As a result, almost every plant that can grow in Wisconsin has found some place to its liking in the ridges. The area is an exquisite natural botanical garden.

But you cannot pitch a tent in a slough. The priceless area was to be leveled. Indeed, the sloughs were being filled and the ridges scalped when Albert Fuller, of the Milwaukee Public Museum, first discovered the impending tragedy. Swamp frogs, turtles, mice and ground-nesting birds would be buried under tons of fill along with those rare plants. The campground would destroy the very thing the campers—at least many of them—were seeking.

Fuller began a verbal and written barrage in defense of the forty-acre plot. He pointed out the folly of destroying such a natural masterpiece. "Some counties would spend millions of dollars to create what nature has given us free at Bailey's Harbor," he declared.

After long arguments, letters in newspapers and public appearances, Fuller finally rallied the support he needed. Persuaded at last, the county Park Commission stopped further development. The bulldozers went on to the next job—and the Ridges became a wildflower sanctuary.

We walked one of the nature trails with Roy Lukes, Ridges naturalist. Little of the hard work showed, of course—the quiet forests, and those mossy pools with their chirping little frogs, fitted the scene exactly. It seemed as if they'd always be there. There was no evidence of the struggles of Albert Fuller and his friends—the many talks at civic and women's clubs; the wheedling of "just one more story" out of the newspapers— and the enthusiasm that caught and spread until the park had grown to over seven hundred acres.

Little effort shows, either, as you enjoy a walk with Ty Baumann, manager of the Bay Beach Wildlife Sanctuary just outside of Green Bay. Yet just before we reached the entrance, we drove past land being cleared for homes and shopping centers. Luckily, the presence of the sanctuary will enhance their value, and now Green Bay is enthusiastically proud of its fine waterfowl refuge.

The big pond and lagoons show no marks of the hard labor that had dug the original little puddle. Nor does Ty himself, softspoken and easygoing, betray the battles he has had over the past few years—one of them an actual struggle for his life with an enraged buck deer.

"It was in the fall rutting season," Ty recalled. "We know that deer can be dangerous and unpredictable as adults, especially during mating season, but none of us dreamed that fellow could make such a lightning change. I had just put out some food for him when he hooked at me—just like that. I grabbed him by the antlers and tried to keep the points away from my body. He pushed and thrashed and I couldn't let go."

Ty's wife, Ida, was in the caretaker's cottage "but with the radio going I didn't hear a thing," she told us. "And there was Ty out there in the deer yard, yelling his head off—and nobody to help him. Finally, when I did hear him, I managed to call one of the men and we fought the deer off."

Luckily, Ty Baumann is a large man, and in good shape from hard work. Otherwise the story might have ended in tragedy.

Ty can chuckle over it now. "It's funny what thoughts go through your mind," he said. "All I could think of was 'what a great movie this would make.' Then, as I got tired, I began to wonder if this was really me, yelling and fighting that deer. I figured out that we pushed each other around for about twenty minutes. My hands were raw and I was so covered with blood that they had to give me a bath at the hospital before they could find how much I'd been hurt."

Fortunately Ty's wounds were not serious. The deer, a magnificent creature weighing 230 pounds, was put in a special yard for safety. Visitors, admiring him through the fence, knew nothing of the struggle that had placed him there.

Other struggles are equally hidden. As we visited a number of wildlife or historical areas over the country, we wondered what stories could be told of the long, often bitter, trail that led to their coming into being. The splendid Picacho Peak State Park, north of Tucson, was such an area, with lofty mountains serving as a background for giant saguaro cactus, and a fascinating nature trail that served as a mini-course on the Arizona of yesterday—telling as it did of former uses of plants and minerals by Indians and settlers. What farsighted people, viewing this land so rich with history and tragedy, set it safely aside from building, development, progress?

Or take the University of California's Kendall-Frost Marsh Preserve on Mission Bay, San Diego—perhaps fifty acres of priceless wetland, where the screams of gulls and the cries of shore birds mingle with the whine of power saws, the growl of derricks and the staccato of the riveters crowding in on three sides as a complex of great new buildings arises. What crystal ball pronounced that this land be set aside before it, too, could be flooded by a tide of concrete that would never recede?

On the east coast, consider the emerald necklace that is the chain of offshore Georgia islands. An increasing number of them have been rendered safe from commercial ravishment by the efforts of one of the most charming and personable women of our entire trip: Mrs. Jane Yarn, wife of Dr. Charles Yarn, an Atlanta surgeon. Yet those quiet islands, with their deer and raccoons and teeming aquatic life, show no evidence of the efforts of Jane and her friends to persuade everybody from the governor's office on down that, as she put it, "if we don't do something concrete today, it'll all be concrete tomorrow."

As a result, the Nature Conservancy—a national group that, among other things, provides temporary funds for such purchases—has effectively secured nearly twenty thousand acres in the area, so that the only cranes and clamshells on the islands will be birds and mollusks, and not heavy equipment.

In our own town in Lincoln, Vermont, a forty-acre hillside still wears its woodland mantle because a handful of people refused to mistake development for progress. Early in the 1960's, before most persons had yet taken alarm at the changes occurring all over the Green Mountain state, Donald Brown and Doran Pierce contemplated the probable future of this village where both had been born.

The old Sargent farm in the center of town looked like a great place for about forty houses, they decided. However, the pines, maples and hemlocks that were there already looked even better to them. Both men had tramped that hillside as boys, and they decided that other boys might like to tramp it, too—no matter what happened to the rest of the town.

They got together with a few of their neighbors and mulled over the idea of buying up the woodland. Once it was acquired, it would make a restful patch of green right in the middle of things. Then it could serve as a nature preserve and a playground for children yet unborn. The land would also afford a wonderful backyard for a number of Lincoln homes that looked right up its slopes.

Joining with other residents, they incorporated under Vermont law as a nonprofit organization. Known as Lincoln Sports, Inc., the group inquired about buying the land. It was, indeed, available—for sixty-six hundred dollars. This represented a tidy sum in those days, especially to a clutch of villagers with no resources of their own.

Nevertheless, they managed to scrape up enough money for a down payment. Then someone suggested that funds might be available from state or government sources. Such a proposal, however, raised those independent Vermont hackles. "No government handouts for us," declared Doran's wife, Enola, who was one of the first directors. "We're safe for a few months with our down payment. Let's see what we can do for ourselves."

Such a proclamation, of course, immediately got Enola the position of treasurer of the infant group. Then they set about finding that sixty-six hundred dollars. They put on food sales, sponsored variety shows, cooked a baked-bean supper for the whole town. They wrote a newsletter to everyone who had been present at the original meeting, enclosing a return envelope "with a stamp licked right onto it so you won't throw it away," as they admitted in the newsletter.

The money came in, all right—several hundred dollars' worth. But it was a far cry from sixty-six hundred. And the months of grace for the down payment were rapidly coming to a close.

Undismayed, the plucky group asked Mrs. Kate Tredennick, owner of the land, for an extension of time. Almost before she could reply, an answer came from another source. One of the newsletters had gone to John and Edith Nuner, who had bought an extinct farm near the property. The tone of the letter tickled them. "Besides," Edith told me some time later, "we hoped to move there some day when John retired, and it'd be nice to have that beautiful forty acres as a neighbor."

So the Nuners offered to lend the necessary money to Lincoln Sports, Inc., on a three-year note—interest free. And, just like that, the villagers had their money.

Some organizations, with the pressure removed, would have relaxed. Not so Lincoln Sports, however. Heartened by this show of faith, they doubled their efforts. Scrounging up local talent, they presented Mary Ellen Chase's hilarious play *Harvey*, even taking it on the road to neighboring towns. They sponsored flea markets, country auctions, movies, dog-sled races. The baked-bean supper had gone well, so they followed it with a turkey supper, a pancake breakfast and, in the spring, a sugar-on-snow party.

This last feat involves heating maple syrup until it will form a soft ball when dropped in water—or a gooey mess of ropy taffy when spread on a dish of snow. Scooped off the snow with a fork and downed with fresh homemade doughnuts—plus a bite of sour pickle to cut the sweetness—sugar-on-snow is a delightful early spring toast to the departing frosts of winter.

With all that activity, victory was only a matter of time. One autumn evening, around a picnic fire at the edge of the river that formed a border of its land, the Lincoln Sports group gathered with the Nuners and a few interested spectators for a note-burning ceremony. They handed the Nuners their check, lit the fire, touched off the promissory note—and everybody celebrated with a hot-dog roast.

The spunky group keeps right on going. Now, several years after that landmark picnic—which was a whole year ahead of the Nuners' deadline, by the way—there's a little rope ski tow on the property, a nature trail through the woods, and an ice skating rink that doubles as a softball field in summer. The rink is flooded on freezing nights by the town's volunteer firemen. Like all the facilities, it's available to anybody who wants to use it, whether they live in Lincoln or not.

As it turned out, the purchase of that land was, indeed, a farsighted move. In Lincoln, as in most other Vermont towns today, the bulldozers are busy. Large-scale construction hews to the mark set by the state's Act 250, of which we spoke earlier, but individual homes spring up like new growth on the slopes and meadows. The occupants of these new homes joyfully tramp that hillside, for it is part of *their* backyard, too.

All because, like a flock of terns on a California beach, or like Willis Combs on his tiny Florida preserve, a handful of Vermonters heard the machinery coming.

CHAPTER ELEVEN

Helping Hands

Y O U C A N N E V E R T E L L about people. They do surprising things. Melvin Allison went around in broad daylight with a flashlight and a mirror on a stick. A respected professor was collared for being a Peeping Tom. And three Ontario women held a prayer meeting in the middle of a field—or was it a crap game? The helicopter pilot above them couldn't be sure.

These are just a few of the people who get into such predicaments because of a very human trait: they cannot turn their backs on a creature in need. In these three cases, the object of concern was one that came perilously close to being done in by the very people who love him most: the farmers and country dwellers. The unfortunate creature is the eastern bluebird.

Most people feel they know the bluebird, even if they have never seen one. A little larger than a sparrow, with an incredibly blue back and a deep rust-colored breast, the bluebird has been the symbol of spring for generations. Its liquid warble echoed the gurgle of melting snow and the *plink* of the maple sap in the buckets. The farmer, hearing the welcome song, knew that planting and fence building and the greening of the land would be only a few days—maybe a few weeks—away.

Unfortunately, that same "spring's work," as the farmer calls it, has become a mounting threat to the bluebird. Favorite bluebird nesting spots are gnarled old apple trees, knotholes in wooden fence posts, decaying trees riddled by woodpeckers. Today the apple orchard is culled and pruned until it practically sparkles. Dying trees are cut before they can become hollow. The wooden fence has given way to the sterile electric fence with its metal posts. Even the few knotholes and hollow stubs left are taken over by the more aggressive house sparrows and starlings.

Farmers, outdoorsmen and ornithologists witnessed the decline of the bluebird with alarm. As time passed, Thoreau's "bird who carries the sky on his back," became only a memory over thousands of square miles from the Atlantic coast to mid-continent. A whole human generation grew up in the 1930's and 1940's knowing the bluebird only in the words of popular songs.

In the habits of the struggling bird, however, lay the key to its salvation. Bluebirds will nest in almost any cavity, big or little, high or low. So, in an effort to rescue the bird from the edge of extinction, its friends began supplying those cavities in the form of nest boxes to take the place of the disappearing hollow trees. Hence the man with the flashlight, the Peeping Tom, the mysterious ladies in the meadow.

Melvin Allison and his flashlight have been familiar to the residents around Decorah, Iowa, for about fifteen years. He and his friends have put up dozens of bluebird boxes. Fitted with a hole exactly an inch and a half in diameter—to keep out the starlings, which are slightly larger—the boxes are nailed to likely-looking posts along fence rows and back roads.

"We try not to place them near buildings," Melvin said, "Or they'll be taken over by house sparrows. And we put a stick in the entrance hole until the first of April so the sparrows, which are here all winter, won't get the jump on the bluebirds."

We asked Mr. Allison about the mirror and flashlight. "Very simple: when I visit the boxes in nesting season I just hold the mirror up near the entrance hole and reflect the flashlight into the box. Then, by angling the mirror right, I can see if the nest is occupied without disturbing it. But I'm getting along in years—eighty-eight now—and my eyes aren't so good. Maybe next year I'll use a periscope."

The supposed Peeping Tom was Professor Alexander Middleton, of the University of Guelph, Ontario. He'd been out behind people's homes, making a bird count with a pair of binoculars. The neighbors, suspicious of his antics, notified the police—who, when they received a satisfactory explanation, doubtless chalked the story up as one more fringe benefit of their calling.

The three ladies discovered by the helicopter pilot were Mrs. Hazel Bird—yes, Bird—and her friends, kneeling while they worked on a nest box attached to a length of plank. Then, setting the plank upright and nailing it to a convenient stump, they'd have another bluebird post.

"The 'copter was on routine duty, inspecting a nearby power line," Mrs. Bird told us. "We were tacking tin cans on the post to keep off marauding cats and other enemies. I've often wondered what he handed in for his report of the day."

Helicopters and predators are not the only unscheduled visitors to those three hundred boxes around Coburg, Ontario. The nests themselves spell "home" for all kinds of birds and animals. Tree swallows and house sparrows are the commonest non-bluebird occupants. Whitefooted mice often fill the box with soft grass and plant down, carefully formed around their pink, helpless babies. Red squirrels, chipmunks and flying squirrels move in when they get the chance. One time Mrs. Bird placed a ladder against a post, opened the front of the box for a look—and took a flying leap out into space. The box was the home of a nest of hornets, every one of them hotly insisting on squatter's rights.

An osprey comes in for a landing in its nest, built on an offshore marker buoy in Chesapeake Bay. In this area and elsewhere, projects aimed at protecting the osprey's pesticide-weakened eggs are helping the threatened fish-eater to hold its own.

Often nest boxes are put up at intervals of about five hundred feet along a country lane or fence row, thus creating a bluebird trail. The dean of such trailmakers is Jack Lane, of Brandon, Manitoba. Sometimes alone, often assisted by his many friends, Canada's "bluebird man" has put up more than four thousand boxes over some eleven hundred miles.

His effort has actually reversed the fortunes of the bluebird in the midsection of the continent and earned Jack Lane an honorary doctorate in laws from Brandon University. So now it's Dr. Jack Lane. You can read about "The Man Who Brought the Bluebirds Back" in an article by Fred McGuinness in the *Reader's Digest* for September, 1973.

Another bird that has been the unscheduled victim of our actions is the "fish hawk," or American osprey. As a child I used to thrill to see the osprey, with its six-foot wingspan, hovering in the air while it searched the surface of Seymour's Pond, near my Connecticut home. Spotting a target, it would fold its wings and plunge into the water. It emerged in a shower of spray with a struggling fish—occasionally so large that the osprey had to tow it ashore.

Fishermen sometimes blame the osprey for their own poor luck—even though the lakes and streams were alive with fish when the first pioneers arrived, and every little pond had its "fish hawk" on a scraggly tree. Now, however, the osprey is in danger, not from irate fishermen, but from pesticide poisoning.

Chemicals, sprayed on the fields and trees, are of many kinds. Some disintegrate rapidly into harmless by-products. Others, however—notably, the chlorinated hydrocarbons such as DDT and Chlordane—remain toxic for years. Washing into streams and lakes, they are taken up through the food chain, passing from one form of life to another until they get to the fish—and to the osprey.

Apparently the adult bird is little affected by the poison in its system. The poison changes the blood chemistry, however, preventing normal calcium deposition in the eggs. The shells of such eggs are fragile, and are often broken by the movements of the brooding bird. As each egg breaks she tosses it out—and ends up sitting on an empty nest.

One person among many worried about the struggle of the osprey is Dr. Mitchell Byrd, of William and Mary College in Williamsburg, Virginia. "The heartbreak of it all," Dr. Byrd told us as we sat and chatted in his laboratory, "is that many of the youngsters in those delicate eggs are apparently normal. If they could only hatch successfully, they'd survive."

The way to load the scales in favor of the osprey, Dr. Byrd reasoned, was to protect the eggs until they hatched. One method of increasing the chance of hatching would be to remove the fragile objects from the nest and brood them in an incubator.

Such a plan was fine except for one small detail: the nest of the average osprey is about as accessible as the roof of a church steeple. Ospreys build in the tops of dead trees, the superstructure of lighthouses, the steel towers of electric transmission lines. Sometimes they build on channel markers and navigation buoys in the water, too, "but it's a snap to reach those nests from a tossing boat compared to climbing a rope hitched to a limb that might break at any moment," Dr. Byrd told us.

"It's all right, by the way, to take those eggs," he added. "As with many birds, the female will produce another clutch if the first one is taken soon after laying. So we watch each hen on the nest until she has laid her eggs and then we do our acrobatic act. This has to be done within the first week or she won't produce any more eggs. But if we're lucky we get two or three eggs, while she goes back and lays that many more."

The eggs take just over thirty days to hatch. "And then we've got the same problem all over again," Dr. Byrd sighed. "Now it's back into that swaying tree with a couple of helpless chicks. Or even if we partially raise the chick on fish, there's still a delicate balancing act to do. By this time the second clutch of eggs has been broken and tossed out. Thus there's usually an empty nest waiting for the chicks. Mother and Father are waiting, too."

This last statement was almost unbelievable to me. From my childhood on a farm, I remembered trying to give orphan chicks to a hen who had lost her own brood; nearly every time she'd refuse to accept the chick, or would even peck it to death if we didn't watch out. But the osprey adult, I learned, makes an ideal foster parent. It looks at that new youngster in the nest, blinks as if to say "where'd *you* come from?"—and then goes out to catch it a fish.

"It's a lot of work," Dr. Byrd agreed, "and hardly worth it except in the case of a threatened species. You have to go out to that nest within a time-bracket of a week, no matter what the weather. And with several dozen nests, spread over half the Chesapeake Bay area, you've got some traveling to do. Rain, wind, hot sun—out you go."

This timetable means that Dr. Byrd and his assistants must get up long before dawn and work until dark. Then they drag home—to repeat the same process the next morning. Someone asked one of his students how long they worked at checking or collecting. "Oh, about twenty-six hours a day," was the weary reply.

All that effort translates into saving one egg for every two collected—the average survival rate for a normal population. "But in this way we make every female do double duty," Dr. Byrd said. "And with a species where every new flying youngster is a headline, it's worth the effort."

While Dr. Byrd's group, the North American Osprey Committee, is trying to save one of the continent's largest hawks, another group is working toward the same result for the swiftest. The peregrine falcon, or duck hawk, is one of the fastest-flying birds in the world, having been clocked at ninety miles per hour in straight flight; twice that speed in a steep dive. Indeed, it is such a feathered bullet that it often just hurtles into its prey in midair, striking it with a clenched fist and allowing the prey to flutter lifelessly to earth.

As with the osprey, the peregrine falcon suffers from a calcium imbalance in the blood, brought about by DDT and other chemicals. The resulting thin-shelled eggs break in the nest. Peregrine falcon nests are even harder to reach than osprey nests, for they are often on ledges that would give the shivers to a mountain goat. Not only that, but there are perhaps fewer than two hundred pairs of breeding peregrines left on the entire continent. Nests of the bird are so rare that to sight a single adult—much less a nest—is, for most birders, a once-in-a-lifetime event.

There are a few of the falcons in captivity, however. Fortunately they take well to handling. Dr. Clayton M. White of Brigham Young University in Provo, Utah, has four pairs of peregrines in a specially-built eyrie on top of the zoology building. Dr. Tom J. Cade, at Cornell, and Robert Berry of Chester Springs, Pennsylvania, have a few more pairs. Dr. White was in Alaska at the time of our visit to Brigham Young University, but Robert Berry's converted barn in Chester Springs is typical of the few eyries where these birds have been successfully bred in captivity.

"We can house up to ten pairs of falcons in these rooms," Bob Berry told us as we peered through one-way glass at two of the rare birds. The female, the larger of the pair, was perhaps two feet long, the male a few inches smaller. The skylight showed their blue-black backs, splotched underparts and dark heads. When they flew to the twenty-foot ceiling of their enclosure we could see the long tail, and the long, swept-back, pointed wings that told of speed, even in such close quarters.

"More than two dozen peregrines were raised in the last

year in the United States and Canada in breeding projects such as these," Bob said. "Ordinarily that'd be a pretty small number, but when you're working with only a handful in the whole world it's a triumph."

The breeding of a bird so wild and free is, indeed, a triumph. The hope of the Peregrine Fund, which is concerned with these and other large hawks, is that the tragic effects of DDT will lessen over the years, and more individuals may be released to their rightful home on those high cliffs.

There are many groups watching over endangered species, both plant and animal. For a hundred dollars you may help the Eagle Valley Environmentalists set aside "An Acre for an Eagle," near Cassville, Wisconsin. This section of the Mississippi River Valley is the major winter roosting area for the entire midwest bald eagle population. Terrence N. Ingram, of Apple River, Illinois, conceived the plan and told others about it. Now churches and schools and other groups from Maine to California have joined hundreds of individuals in purchasing about a third of the needed thousand acres thus far.

In Michigan's southern peninsula the Michigan Audubon Society, U.S. Forest Service, and Michigan Department of Natural Resources have combined in a last-ditch effort to rescue one of America's rarest songbirds. The Kirtland's warbler, whose total known population numbers some four hundred birds, nests in just a handful of Michigan counties. It has steadily lost ground due to its need for just the right nesting habitat: Christmas-tree-sized jackpines. It also suffers from the parasitic habits of the brown-headed cowbird, which lays its eggs in the nests of smaller birds.

Why the warbler builds only in those small jackpines is not known. But when the pines get beyond eighteen feet tall, the warbler moves on. So, to keep young trees in production, a small area of old pines is burned each year after the nesting season. The heat causes the tough scales of the pine cones to relax—and within two years a new pine forest is on the way.

Peg and I visited the Kirtland's area just at the start of the nesting season with Dr. George Wallace and his wife, of Grayling, Michigan. "Now be sure to listen sharp," Martha Wallace cautioned. "This is the chance of a lifetime. You don't want to miss it."

We drove slowly along a gravel road, our ears straining for the slightest chirp. Never having heard a Kirtland's warbler, we didn't quite know what to expect. I knew what the sound was supposed to be like, but only from a description. We hardly dared to breathe, so fearful were we of missing the song.

As the car approached a grove of trees of the right size and species, George nodded his head toward a dense clump. "Now really listen. I think there's one over there. Don't miss it."

As we drew near the clump I gripped the edge of the car window in my effort to catch the first notes of the elusive song. Doubtless they'd be low and sad for a bird so near extinction.

Suddenly the June air fairly exploded. Three loud, pronounced notes burst from the clump, followed by a lilting burble. Abruptly it stopped.

I looked at Martha Wallace. She was smiling. Listen sharp, indeed! How could you ever shut that sound out of your hearing?

The song rang out again. And again. We got out of the car and walked to the edge of the road. The grounds themselves were off limits, so there'd be no danger of disturbing the bird's nest or its activities. But with binoculars we were close enough, anyway.

Scarce twenty feet away sat the warbler, its gray-blue back, streaked with black, contrasting with the yellow of its undersides. It had a black mask, plus splotchy black marks on its breast. One of the continent's rarest songbirds—about as shy as a robin in a rosebush!

After we'd listened to the warbler, photographed it and put its voice on tape, the Wallaces took us to see one or two other singing males. Then we drove to some burned-over pine land. Already, even though the burn had been done just the previous year, we could spot tiny pines poking up through the blueberries and ferns. Then we visited the second part of the two-pronged effort on behalf of the Kirtland's: the cowbird trap.

Cowbirds, like the European cuckoo, lay their eggs in the nests of other birds. Ordinarily this is one of the natural processes whereby the host species is kept in check. The rawboned interloper, hatching quickly, soon shoves the rightful nestlings over the side. "With the Kirtland's warbler the cowbird seems to have a special vendetta," George told us. "Instead of one out of five or ten, say, the cowbird finds almost every Kirtland's nest. With a hundred pairs of the warblers nesting, you'll merely raise a hundred new cowbirds."

The current answer to the problem is the cowbird trap—a large enclosure screened on top and sides. It is baited with food, plus a few of the last catch of cowbirds. Other cowbirds come to join the party, forcing against the screen until they find a one-way opening. Once inside they find plenty of food, but no exit.

The captured cowbirds are removed from the Kirtland's nesting area, to the tune of about three thousand a year. This, plus the jackpine program, resulted in a 1973 increase of eight percent, or a total of 432 Kirtland's.

There are so many other groups, large and small, each with its special concern, that as you learn about them you realize there is, indeed, another side to the story of man's collision course with nature. We are doubtless selfish, greedy, grasping, and all the rest. But we are also human. Being human, we come up with an organization to save the Tallgrass Prairie, for instance, while another group hopes to preserve the splendid little Tule elk of California.

Add a few more—at first sight unrelated but all on the bright side of the coin. There's my friend, John Hansel, of Harrisville, New Hampshire, for instance, whose Elm Research Institute is hard at work on a remedy for Dutch Elm Disease. Or consider the Frenchman River Valley in Saskatchewan, near the small town of Val Marie. The valley contains a colony of black-tailed prairie dogs—listed as the only legally protected home of these playful rodents in all of Canada.

Top it off with James Butler, of the Manti-LaSal National Forest in Utah, who took us on a wild truck ride through Straight Canyon, where we witnessed a unique plan for cooperation with wildlife. There the deer and elk, coyotes and jackrabbits, dispossessed by the damming of water for Joe's Valley Reservoir, are now moving at their own speed to an adjoining two-thousand-acre "mitigation area." Larger than their original valley, this area is managed so as to produce even more food and shelter than their former range. It's also the first place of its kind where the federal government has actually found new homes for animals evicted by its own actions.

So there may be a heart even in official government policy, as well as in some private citizen who's concerned about bluebirds or falcons or prairie dogs. Which, actually, shouldn't be a complete surprise: after all, governments are composed of people.

And you can never tell about people. They do surprising things.

CHAPTER TWELVE

A Bear
in the Bedroom

''M A N ' S   F I R S T   P E T ''—that phrase can set you thinking. Was the first pet a jungle fowl that came for lunch—and stayed beyond dessert? A wildcat kitten? Some pre-raccoon cub whose antics kept it off the bill of fare?

Nobody knows. Most likely it was not a pet at all. Many people feel it could have been just a wolf pup, something like those of John Harris, whom we met in Chapter Four. The pup may have been so good at begging—and dodging sticks and stones—that early cave dwellers allowed it to remain.

It has been here ever since. Sometimes it still resembles that first wolf—it may even carry a bit of the blood of its wild ancestors. Such is the case with our own pup. She is the second-generation offspring of an alliance between a Canadian sled dog and a captive timber wolf. (Wolves, it seems, are often mated with sled dogs; the resulting offspring is vigorous and hardy, with the urge to go that last mile at the end of a long run.)

Our Laska has the coloration of the Siberian husky but the general build of one of John Harris's wolves. She acts a bit like a wolf, too: howling instead of barking, and trying to get in front of a ball and "head it off" when you throw it, rather than chase it directly.

Laska also seeks close personal contact by pressing against you and gently licking you in a gesture of togetherness that her blood remembers dimly from the wolf pack. Not a fawning, cringing lick, by the way, but a companionable, dry-tongued greeting that leaves no trace—except for the consternation on the face of the person favored by such attention.

Most of the time, however, Laska is safe behind her fence. We wouldn't have her at all, much as we have learned to love her, except that we felt we needed a wolf—or near-wolf—to help publicize the debut of a book I had written. The book, *Animals Nobody Loves*, starts out with a chapter on wolves.

Laska was just a puppy then. Somehow, after our publicity effort was over, she was still around. She has been around ever since. We made her a big enclosure to run in, for, even though she is only a quarter-wolf, she could never be a household pet. A wild animal should forever remain just that: a wild animal.

It is this wildness that has caused so many creatures to be taken in as pets. Sometimes they are kept as an exotic status symbol: the cheetah at the end of a leash on Park Avenue, for instance. Other times they reflect our yearning for a touch of the outdoors, even if it's only a salamander in a terrarium. Some people I know kept a skunk, hidden from all but a few close friends, high in an apartment building in the Bronx.

That skunk was complete and unabridged, in full possession of two efficient spray guns, by the way. However, "she hasn't ever made a mistake—yet," as her master bravely assured me the last time I saw him.

Often, however, some "mistake" does occur. Ricky Raccoon feels the urge of the mating season and suddenly bites

the hand that feeds him. Jasmine *does* let go with her atomizer
—just a quick puff, but it's enough to empty the whole four-
teenth floor.

Maybe the mistake is of another kind. A young squirrel is
orphaned by somebody's cat, perhaps, or a bird shatters a
wing against a window. Such waifs need instant help. Most
people are not equipped to care for them, but they often try.
Usually it means curtains for the unhappy creatures. However, if the enterprise is a success it's often only a matter of
time before the word gets around.

"You did so well with the baby opossum that fell out of its
mother's pocket," says a visitor with a mysterious box, "that
we just knew you'd be able to care for this wounded snapping
turtle."

After the turtle comes a rabbit, perhaps, or a swallow that
lost its tail. Before long, the person who started it all is running a veritable zoo. And I speak from experience. Peg and I
have granted asylum and therapy to three hundred such
foundlings over the years.

Thus it was with more than ordinary curiosity that we
searched the country for people who, like us, cannot say "no"
to a creature in need.

One of the most memorable visits of our trip was the result of
sheer chance. In Sanibel, Florida, Peg and I noticed a red step-
van with a sign that interested us: CROW Wildlife Rescue.

The van got away before we could apprehend it, but we
saw it again the following day. I managed to flag it down, and
introduced myself to the woman who was driving it. In answer to my request, she said she was on an emergency call.
"But follow me," she said, "and you'll see what CROW is all
about."

We followed her on her current errand of mercy: a sparrow that had built a home in a fire alarm and had been
knocked silly when the bell was tested. Then, motioning us to

A bathtub scene with young pelican, set at Rosemary Collett's Venice, Florida, home, which serves as a halfway-house for disabled, abandoned or otherwise abused wildlife.

continue, our guide from CROW took us—and the sparrow—to her backyard menagerie.

Her name was Shirley Walter. She and Jessie Dugger ran a wildlife art gallery, known as Fur, Feathers and Scales, in Sanibel. Given their special interest, it was only natural that creatures down on their luck should be brought to the two women.

"Sanibel seems to have more than its share of such animals," Shirley said. "Or maybe people just see them more. The place is overrun with tourists all winter, so any wounded bird or animal will be discovered. Besides, a lot of our visitors are fishermen. Tangled fishline is one of the worst booby traps ever invented. A creature gets a leg or a wing—or even its head—caught in a loop of the stuff, and the first thing you know it's tied in knots."

CROW—Care and Rehabilitation of Wildlife, Inc.—had been in existence for nearly five years at the time of our visit. The animal compound included a fenced enclosure nearly the size of a tennis court in Shirley and Jessie's backyard. It had a small natural pool and several huts for shelter. The compound was populated with a variety of birds. The more exuberant of these, which might have escaped over the four-foot fence, were kept in roomy cages in another part of the yard.

We gazed at some two dozen gulls, terns, pelicans and ducks in CROW's enclosure—all in various stages of repair and rehabilitation. One brown pelican detached himself from the crowd and waddled gravely in our direction.

"Here comes Austin," Shirley said. "We've had him about as long as any bird in the place."

She proceeded to tell us Austin's story. He had been taken from his parents by well-intentioned people, but was abandoned when the novelty wore off. Brought to Jessie and Shirley, he was nearly starved.

"Over the next couple of months," Shirley said, "he learned to fly. We released fish in a swimming pool and he discovered how to catch them. Then he took to the beach, but he hung around for a couple of months waiting for us to show up with morning and afternoon snacks."

Austin, who had been nuzzling the pail of fish Shirley had brought out from the house, turned his head a moment. We could see that one eye was injured.

"He was so tame that anybody could walk up to him on the beach," Shirley continued. "For reasons known only to them, some people clipped his wings. Others nearly put out his eye. After his wings got better he flew away, and we thought we'd seen the last of him. But six months later he was picked up on the mainland. So now he's here for good. He's much too people-oriented to be on his own."

She gave a few fish to Austin, then tossed the rest to the other birds. One pelican had lost a wing. "That's Adam," Shirley said. "At least we *think* it's Adam. Austin has taken up with him lately. They're together much of the time. Perhaps they have something going whereby we'll have to change one's name."

We met the other residents: Susie, the pelican whose pouch had been slashed ("Dr. Phillis Douglas in Fort Myers had to sew it up three times—we felt like fixing it with one of those iron-on patches"); Happy, the young red-tailed hawk; Brownie, the owl, whose wing was shattered by a shotgun, and assorted other star boarders. Some were almost ready for release, while many would remain for the rest of their lives.

"We're growing all the time," Shirley said. "Now we're dickering for more land. If Austin and Adam get serious it'd sure be nice to have a place where one of them—whichever is which—could lay some eggs. It'd be a 'first' in captivity, as far as we know. And brown pelicans are an endangered species."

Back in that wildlife art gallery, Jessie Dugger echoed her thoughts. "CROW is an official nonprofit corporation," Jessie said. "We need fencing and more flight cages, and a pump for

our pool. We need a proper rescue vehicle, too. It's a little
tricky carrying a fragile ceramic raccoon from our gift shop
on the seat when the real thing is in there, too, roaming all
over the car."

The Misses Walter and Dugger also haul exhibits and display materials around in that van. A major part of their task is
to help people know and understand birds and animals. In this
effort they sometimes call on the Felicidades Wildlife Foundation in Venice, Florida. The Foundation is actually George
and Rosemary Collett, their daughter, Janice, and a host of
friends.

It was the Colletts to whom Austin the pelican was taken
when he was found near their home. "After he left Sanibel he
ended up on Boca Grande, thin and weak," Rosemary told us.
"We picked him up, had him here for a while, and happened
to be talking on the phone with Jessie and Shirley about a one-
eyed pelican. 'My God!' Jessie said. 'That sounds like Austin!'
So the girls drove up from Sanibel and picked him up. They
were delighted to have him back. You never saw such a
reunion!"

Like their island neighbors at CROW, the Colletts have a
yard full of birds and animals. George, a retired airline agent,
may don a heavy jacket and leather gloves to subdue a fright-
ened great blue heron, for instance; that six-inch beak can put
out an eye. His wife and daughter supply the gentle feminine
touch with the constant stream of animals—from skunks to
seagulls—that pass through their kitchen, their yard, even
their bathtub.

While saving little lives is one task of the Colletts' nonprofit
foundation, a second task is the education of others. The
Colletts are on the move much of the time. They visit schools,
service clubs, conventions and churches. With them go color
slides of their animals, plus a member of the current crop.
One time it may be a friendly skunk; another, a baleful owl or
a drowsy tortoise.

Rosemary's book about it all, *My Orphans of the Wild*, has recently been published by Lippincott. It's a delight to read ("I tell my houseguests, 'The bathroom is first door on the left, and be careful not to upset the pelican, please,' "), and you learn much valuable information ("Baby rabbits do not want to be burped"; grasping an otter is "like trying to hold a wet noodle"; and "opossums are dumb, dumb, dumb.")

The Colletts have been featured on TV in the *CBS Evening News*, and Charlie Briggs's article on their whole fascinating array appeared in the November, 1972 issue of *Lady's Circle* magazine. Its title? You guessed it: "Rosemary's Babies."

Some day I'd like to get Rosemary Collett together with Katharine McKeever. It would be fun to turn on a tape recorder, start the movie camera—and let the two of them go. Oh, yes, there should be a few animals. Any animals will do, doubtless, but if I had plenty of film and tape I'd be sure to include a few owls.

Kay lives in Vineland Station, Ontario, twenty miles west of Niagara Falls. Owls are her specialty. Like Rosemary Collett, Kay delights in her work. So enthusiastic is she that wildlife specialists, wardens, local park and forest authorities, veterinarians and her many friends turn to her for owl expertise. Complete strangers often telephone or pay a visit. "We saw your television review on owls," they might say, "and there's this big bird in our hollow tree. . . ."

Sometimes they bring her the owl. With the exception of the saw-whet and screech owl among the commoner kinds in her area, most of the owls are large enough to make tempting targets. Then, belatedly realizing he's wounded a bird protected by law, the shooter materializes at Kay's door: "Here's an owl, Mrs. McKeever. Some hunter must have shot it."

Although to most of us even a single owl would be an event, Kay has an incredible six dozen of them. "We have sixty-nine owls on the premises at the moment," she wrote to me. "But it's not really that many. Twenty are due for release in the spring."

Kay doesn't merely collect these birds as objects, however. She makes every effort to learn about them. She tries to adjust her ways to theirs, to make things comfortable for those that must remain with her for the rest of their lives. Such efforts sometimes take amazing patience and unusual skill—and produce surprising results.

Birds—almost any birds, from canaries to cranes—are wary of anything that comes from above. Few of their perils approach from beneath them. This is true in the case of owls, too. So Kay greets new arrivals in an unorthodox way: on her hands and knees.

The owl, instead of being alarmed at such an apparition, merely watches it with interest. This odd creature on all fours must be some kind of sweater-clad cow, perhaps, or a rabbit too big for a meal. Kay used this technique with one magnificent snowy owl.

> I entered the cage on hands and knees, keeping my head lower than hers and my eyes averted, and when close enough, offered her the top of my head for grooming [a preening motion of the beak]. This act of inferiority, or obsequiousness, allows her to maintain her position of superiority without feeling threatened by me and she is greatly reassured, despite the strange, new surroundings.
>
> In this way I am able to offer her food (which she would prefer to take from my "face," but will accept from my hand) and to give her an injection of penicillin—only momentarily alarming. With large owls, needing both food and handling within a day of arrival, this little routine is enacted over and over again, with some variations, year in and year out, and has never yet failed to soften or break down entirely the initial barriers of fear and self defense.

For some reason, however, the same ruse doesn't work with juvenile large owls, big enough to fly. Perhaps, as with many other adolescents, they are unsure of themselves, and do not want anything to do with such a zany creature. They may escape to the far corner of the cage, raking Kay's head with their talons on the way. One ornithologist tried the hands-and-knees approach on a juvenile owl in a large flight cage with a tree in it—and ended up climbing the tree to retrieve his toupee.

Marge Facklam, whose nature books for children I have long enjoyed, told me how Kay once contracted with two workmen to build a large platform for owls in a tree. The more portly of the pair climbed up the ladder and into the tree, some fifty feet above Kay's head. She sent twigs up to him and had him build a "nest," with the largest twigs on the bottom, smaller ones on top of these—and so on, until the smallest were in place.

"Now," she called up to him, "make a depression."

"A *what?*"

"A depression."

"How do I do that?"

At this point the workman on the ground, doubtless thoroughly exasperated with the whole affair, spoke up. "Oh, you know how! Just plank your arse down and wiggle it around!"

The men, by the way, never sent Kay a bill for the job. When she tried to pay them later, they refused. "No, ma'am! We got a lot of mileage from the story at the local bar. We had too much fun saying to people, 'You wouldn't guess what we did at this gal's place!' "

Refuges like Kay's are scattered all over the continent. We learned of Roy Ivor near Toronto, for instance, whose Winding Lane Sanctuary receives some fifteen hundred birds and other creatures a year. We met Liz Black, just outside Oklahoma City, whose adventures began with a fuzzy young egret ("he looked like an overgrown Q-tip") and haven't ended yet. ("You should see my house now—it looks as if a tornado came in, loved it, and stayed.")

We chatted past midnight with Tom and Sandy Rush, of Winnipeg, and stayed several days with George and Gladys Munford of Grayling, Michigan—two husband-wife teams with an amazing fund of continent-wide information on everything from Manitoba moose to California condors.

We even had supper with a Nevada rancher who live-traps, tags and releases coyotes, but won't let me tell his name "or my neighbors'll get up a lynching party."

We also met the man who slept with a bear. A full-grown, unchained bear that he had met only three hours previously.

The man's name is Carl Marty. His resort at Three Lakes, in northern Wisconsin, is sought out by senators, governors, movie stars and sports heroes when they want to rough it— but not too rough—on the golf links, nature trails, or guided boat tours provided at fabulous Northernaire resort.

The Northernaire is sought out by wild animals, too. Hundreds of them have wandered out from the woods and streams of the Wisconsin lake country to a warm welcome by "Mr. Conservation" plus his human guests, and—until she died of old age—his dog, Ginger.

It was a dog who began it all. Carl, walking along the grounds surrounding the cabin where he lived before the Northernaire was built, saw his dog playing in the gloom of night ahead of him. At first he thought Rusty was frolicking with another dog, but as he looked closer he discovered Rusty's companion was a fox.

The scene intrigued Carl. Although he had been passionately fond of all animals, wild and tame, as a youngster, this was the first time he had ever seen a fox do anything but run from a dog—even a silky little spaniel like Rusty.

Soon fox and dog parted company. But Carl couldn't forget the sight. Perhaps, if Rusty had a way with one fox, he might have a similar effect on others. So Carl, delighted to have an excuse to indulge his childhood love of animals, got a young fox to see what would happen.

The experiment was an instant hit—with dog, fox and man. Such a hit, indeed, that when Carl was offered two more of these little wild canines he accepted at once.

Thus it began. Local sportsmen, outdoorsmen, and conservation officials presented Carl with one creature after another. He never caged or confined any of them—except, perhaps, for a brief period for treatment or recuperation. They were free to wander as they pleased—even into Carl's cabin and, later, when the Northernaire was completed, around the newly-built resort hotel itself. Guests, of course, were delighted with the chance to pet a halfgrown fawn, or to be nuzzled by a wet, friendly otter.

Eventually the list of wildlings at the Northernaire read like an animal encyclopedia. They were greeted and suitably mothered by Rusty's daughter, Ginger, who became the star of Carl's book *Ginger and her Woodland Orphans*. Through the years Ginger's wilderness protégés have included such personalities as Narcissus the skunk, Snoopy the Raccoon, Bopper Beaver, Lulu the wolf, Orphan Annie Fox, Albert the bear cub and Ouch the porcupine.

Following Rusty and Ginger were two St. Bernards in succession: Bernese I and Bernese II. Huge as these dogs are, they were able to calm the fears of even an orphan chipmunk—bowling it over with a great, warm tongue in the process.

Oh, yes. The bear. Carl told us about it as we sat on the spacious terrace and watched Bernese II playing with a foundling we ourselves had rescued on our trip: Alice the turtle, stranded in the middle of an interstate highway in Kansas.

"The bear's name was Tanga," Carl recalled. "She was brought to me when fully grown. She had been chained all her life and, while not vicious, insisted on having her own way. She had the muscle to back up her ideas, too."

He scratched his thinning white hair, smiling to himself as he considered the whole affair. "The night the people brought her, I just turned her loose in the cabin with me. Some people would say this was a foolish move, but I am fully convinced that if man goes ten percent of the way, the animal will go the other ninety. Here was a chance to prove it."

The bear wandered around, exploring the cabin, finally making her way out through the open door. Carl followed, walking along with her for a while. When he turned to go back to the cabin she accompanied him.

"And I'll be darned if, when she got back inside, she didn't climb right up on the bed," he chuckled. It was bedtime, anyway, so I just curled up beside her."

It was, he admits, an eventful night. Bears apparently sprawl when they sleep, and every now and again he woke to find a big, furry arm across his chest. "But I just lay quietly until she shifted, and then I shifted, too."

They both made it through the night unscathed, and Tanga found a den of her own the following day.

Eventually Carl's cabin was turned completely over to the animals. Then "the St. Francis of the North Country," as author Sterling North has called him, moved into his present quarters—a small room at the spacious Northernaire. To help his wild friends use their home to the fullest, he cut holes in the walls and floor and set a tree trunk in the living room of the old cabin. We saw movies taken in the cabin after dark: skunks coming up through the floor, deer and foxes eating a mixed meal from the same dish, and raccoons clowning all over that tree trunk.

But no Tanga. After she had suitably investigated the grounds of Northernaire—including the stage of its night club, where she performed like an old trouper—the bear wandered off into the woods.

Perhaps she's there now. "But if you see her," says Carl, "don't invite her to be your guest for the night. She snores something awful."

CHAPTER THIRTEEN

Ninety-Seven-Pound Weakling

NOT EVERY captive animal has the good fortune to meet with the like of Rosemary Collett, or Carl Marty, or the girls from CROW. We have seen plenty of misfits like the apartment-bound skunk that I mentioned a few pages back..

There is a woman in Massachusetts who keeps an otter in a child's swimming pool in her basement, for instance. And I reached through the heavy wire mesh on the front of a garage in New Hampshire and scratched the ears of a full-grown lion. His master's relatives in Detroit had bought him as a cub. When he outgrew their apartment, he was shipped east to his two-car garage.

You don't need an uncle in Detroit, however, if your heart is set on a misfit of your own. I know of a local pet shop that will procure me a skunk, properly censored and guaranteed to be as tame as a kitten. Price, fifty dollars. For ten dollars less I can get a raccoon.

Varying other amounts will get me a fox, crow, muskrat or woodchuck "so you can celebrate groundhog day in your own home," as the catalogue says. And last winter at a sportsman's show a gentleman sidled up and offered me a cougar kitten—"live delivery guaranteed, my friend"—as if he were selling French postcards. I could have had it for two hundred dollars.

Peg and I have had the chance to become impromptu dealers ourselves. Our experiences with animals have led others to wish to share in the fun. Following publication of my book *How Do You Spank A Porcupine?* I had numerous requests for a baby porky—even though the book tries to make it clear that our own small Piney was a starving orphan when we found him, alone and bewildered, in a woodland.

Quite rightly, the law frowns on the keeping of wild animals as pets. Wild animals you caught yourself, that is. In many parts of the United States and Canada, however, you can purchase a native animal from a recognized dealer, although you cannot go out and capture—or rescue—one in the wild.

Apparently it's the bill of sale that makes the difference. The dealer is a businessman who pays taxes and buys a license to keep and sell wild creatures. He knows and cares about his animals.

Or at least he's *supposed* to. Sometimes he does a great job; I know a pet dealer in Connecticut who keeps his charges in airy, well-ventilated cages. If you buy so much as a hamster you get a free booklet and a ten-minute lecture on the care and feeding of the durable little rodent. The proprietor takes your name and address, too, so when you leave the store you feel as if you're walking out of an adoption agency.

That is how one well-run pet shop operates. The pet business, however, is a big, sprawling enterprise. Doubtless it will get larger as our natural areas shrink and man yearns for some contact, however small, with the vanishing wilderness. In their attempt to serve this need, some dealers are too busy to give proper attention to their charges. Others just do not care.

Supposedly, there are authorities, public and private, who look over the dealer's shoulder to see that he toes the mark.

Agriculture and Conservation officials control his operating permit. The Health Department worries about his impact on human sanitation. If his cages are excessively foul, or his charges are deprived of reasonably humane treatment, he'll have to surrender his license and turn in his animals. In addition, irresponsible dealers gain an unsavory reputation with groups such as the American Feline Society and the American Kennel Club. Ideally, it seems, animal dealers are subject to strict oversight and control.

In fact, of course, supervision of animal dealers falls far short of this ideal. Authorities themselves may be busy, indifferent, or bogged down with paper work. Such may be the case all the way from the appropriate government agencies to the American Society for the Prevention of Cruelty to Animals (ASPCA). This beleaguered front-runner labors under a whole gamut of conditions from apathy to downright hostility.

"Sometimes we have no choice," a field worker for an ASPCA unit in New York City told me, "but to grease the squeaky wheel, and hope the other wheels are all right. I spent this morning on a complaint thirty miles from here. This afternoon I'm headed off in the other direction. Tomorrow I'm in court. Sometime I've got to sit down and write out a sheaf of reports."

He shrugged. "So unless there's a pressing reason to visit an animal dealer or pet store, it'll be a long time before they see my smiling face. We have to depend on the general public to keep us up to date."

Often that's the way things stand. The "general public" assumes there will be adequate inspection, while legal and enforcement agencies rely on the same general public to tell them what needs inspecting. In the process, sometimes, everybody's business becomes nobody's business.

But Marie-Louise Poisson of Worcester, Massachusetts, is not the general public. Not by a long shot. This perky five-foot housewife is ninety-seven pounds of perseverance. As the result of casual inquiries about pets in her area she made a few unsettling discoveries. At first they were unsettling just to her, but the more she thought about them the more she worried. Then she translated those worries into action.

It all began when Marie-Louise acquired a small raccoon in the early days of summer. He was an engaging little fellow, even if he was an orphan: mischievous eyes in a black mask, almost-human little hands, roly-poly body and ringed tail. He adopted his new family at once and took to his foster home like a puppy. As with most raccoons, he was naturally housebroken—at least to the extent of using a certain favorite corner for his personal needs. He was curious about everything. He opened boxes, rummaged in closets, poked underneath buildings. He'd stretch an inquisitive arm into a knothole as far as it would go just to explore its hidden depths.

Someone reminded the Poissons of the edict against keeping wild animals in captivity. "But the problem wasn't one of *keeping* him," Marie-Louise told me. "It was how we'd ever get rid of him when we wanted to. That little fellow knew a good thing when he saw it."

At any rate, the time came for the Poissons to take their vacation. This, they decided, was when they'd part with little Frewfie. The authorities at nearby Wachusetts Wildlife Meadows accepted him as a guest. They helped wean him from civilized foods to frogs, berries and other wild edibles. But the family missed him, and when the vacation ended Marie-Louise decided to see about replacing him with a non-contraband raccoon from a licensed dealer.

This is where the pepper hit the stove. I had had occasional letters from Marie-Louise about her raccoon; now the mail came up from Worcester in a barrage. I'll give you some of the highlights, beginning in early September:

September 2—"I checked with the Fish and Game people

This raccoon has more ample space over which to range than other unfortunate creatures that Marie-Louise Poisson worked to rescue from dirty, confined quarters provided by uncaring "pet dealers." (PHOTO BY BEN ROGERS, COURTESY OF THE ROTHER STUDIO OF PHOTOGRAPHY, MIDDLEBURY, VERMONT)

at the Department of Natural Resources. They told me that one could buy a raccoon from a licensed breeder after obtaining a permit from their Bureau in Boston. They sent me an application which I immediately filled and returned along with my three-dollar check. Now I have to wait until the local law enforcement person inspects my premises to see if everything is O.K. before I can have the permit.

"During this time I contacted some people on the list which accompanied the application, a list of licensed dealers and breeders.

"One place was a wild animal farm; animals such as skunks, honey bears, ringtailed cats, a fox, are maintained in really small wooden boxes, with hardly space to turn around in. There is no bedding, the floors are sodden, the quarters generally dark and fetid. The raccoons were quartered with snapping turtles; the beaver in the neighboring cement-plus-water enclosure had his head hanging down between his legs and stayed that way; he looked as if he were dying.

"But all this was a comparative paradise to what I saw yesterday. I visited the farm of a breeder in a small town. This man had three pens with raccoons. All were unbelievably filthy, and the only water available was in rusty tubs. The water itself was black with a scum on the surface.

"One of the pens was of heavy mesh, small, situated in the direct sun with no roof for shade. The animals had a conglomeration of old cans and a small doghouse in which to get away from the sun. The second pen was in the semi-shade, made up of old pieces of lumber with no openings except for the screen door, so the interior was quite dark. Also incredibly filthy. This pen had four or five full-grown animals in it.

"The third pen, hidden in the back, was totally unbelievable. It was also made of haphazard pieces of old lumber, lots of jagged edges, but this one had no openings whatsoever because even the door was all of one piece. There was no air, no light, complete darkness—and the filth. There were three males cowering in this one."

Marie-Louise inquired of the Massachusetts Department of Natural Resources office about this second pet dealer. How was it that such a place was licensed by the Department?

Well, the spokesman on the other end of the line said after a pause, it didn't seem that he *was* licensed. Not for the current year, anyway. Four years ago he'd been inspected, but not since then, even though he was on the Department's list of animal dealers.

Incredulous, Marie-Louise demanded that the Department take a look for itself. Then, just to be sure she wasn't going off the deep end, she visited three other listed dealers so she'd have a basis for comparison. "If I find that these people give an O.K. to that man," she wrote, practically striking sparks from her typewriter, "I guess I'll go right to the papers and see if they can do something."

Four days later she wrote to me again, while waiting for the State to make its inspection. Her letter is a study in frustration:

September 12—"I did call a few people who I thought would be very interested as they are persons of local influence and highly placed. One man especially dotes on raccoons. The first man expressed sympathy ('That's a shame.') and gave me three names to call, asking me to let him know later how I made out.

"The raccoon lover also expressed some outrage; he said he would mull it over and then call me to tell me what he planned to do. Since I never heard from man #2, I called him during the week, and he told me he was trying to get hold of the Chief of Police in that town and that he would call me back when he had something. He never called back, so scratch him."

Marie-Louise telephoned a prominent veterinarian. More outrage. "And I'll certainly look into it the next time I'm down that way," he sputtered.

Then she started on the three names she had been given by her first contact. All three were top-drawer men, but she persisted until she got through their secretaries and had them on the phone. The first said such problems were "not our bailiwick; call the Massachusetts SPCA [which she had long since contacted]." The second was an editorial writer for a large newspaper. "What do you want *me* to do about it?" this gentleman barked as he slammed down the phone.

The third man was in a position as high as Marie-Louise could go without ringing up the governor. In the course of their conversation, the man showed skepticism and amusement that she had found "some sub-standard places." Then he implied something that had begun to bother Marie-Lousie herself: that she was some kind of a crank.

Nobody seemed to get excited. Several persons had wished Marie-Louise well—said they'd even hold her coat. One had as much as told her she was off her rocker. "And not *one* of them has been down to see what I'm talking about," she told me on the phone, "while those animals sit in their filthy pens."

Wondering how best to help Marie-Louise from here in Vermont, I made a couple of telephone calls of my own. But I had no friends near the town where the offending animal farm was located, so I got only promises, too. Besides, all I really had was her word about the whole affair. Perhaps she was, indeed, out in left field.

Marie-Louise had no intention of quitting. She visited five more animal farms. Now she was convinced that she was on the right track. She spoke to a man who had an outdoor television show; he asked her to keep in touch "and let him know what I accomplished because he didn't like to think of animals being kept in squalor." She made a personal appearance at the Department of Natural Resources offices. Her children had gone on that first traumatic visit to the pens; she couldn't let them down, either. Somewhere, somehow, there must be somebody to help her.

Three weeks passed. Marie-Louise had wanted to send a fiery letter to the editor ("two dozen letters if I need to!") but determined to wait until the Department of Natural Resources had had the chance to take action. "If I'm a little incoherent," she wrote, "I beg your indulgence. I'm awfully tired and I must have lost at least fifty pounds after logging perhaps a couple of hundred miles and contemplating the arrival of a phone bill which will be at least one thousand dollars."

Finally her break came. On September 21, nearly a month after she had first discovered the plight of those hapless animals, she sent me the news. A few days before, an official from the Department of Natural Resources had paid the long-hoped-for visit to the animal dealer in question. The official was apalled at the state of the whole place. "He expressed great dismay at the conditions he found there," Marie-Louise wrote. "He gave the man two days to get things cleaned up, or else. Evidently he returned after the two days were up and had the man knock out a wall in the total-darkness shed, clean the place up and supply fresh water."

Vindication at last. More important, those unhappy creatures would have a little breathing room and a drink of fresh water. The official promised he'd be back periodically to check on the condition of the animals.

Marie-Louise followed up with visits of her own. Her letters from early October to mid-November told of several drives out to the animal farm. "I got up my courage and went twice myself," she wrote. "Once I sent some friends because I felt that if I showed my face again, I'd get a fanny full of buckshot."

Now, in looking back at it, Marie-Louise marvels that a plain housewife could have mounted such a campaign. Her friends, her neighbors, even her family regarded her with astonishment. She has not won a clear victory yet, for her struggle unearthed as many problems as it solved. But she shook them up in Boston and got a mess cleaned up. Moreover, she struck a blow for what she believed.

Marie-Louise's persistence and final justification reminded me of a remark by Abraham Lincoln. "To remain silent when they should speak out," he said, "makes cowards of men." And whatever other failures she admitted in all those many notes to me, lack of courage was not one of them. Marie-Louise Poisson has more than enough grit for someone twice her size.

One result of the Case of the Crowded Cages, however, leaves me a bit at a loss, even though I cheer for the housewife with the strength of her convictions:

I am sure going to miss those weekly letters.

The oak falls with a mighty crash, Carlyle said, but it sows its acorns silently. Marie-Louise Poisson makes our hundredth acorn. Or thereabouts. Go back and count them if you wish: each one has had a positive impact on the world about him. They've struggled in their own small ways to bring hope to our land and its living things. Few of them, as I said at the outset, will ever make the newspapers. Many will be astonished to find themselves in this book. They range all the way from a grandmotherly bird enthusiast in a darkened kitchen to a tankful of Marines gawking at a spunky little bird that dared that tank to rumble one inch closer.

Scarcely cast in the same mold, it is true. But they have one thing in common: A faith in tomorrow. They refuse to believe that the plants and animals, soils and people of this wobbly old world are licked.

Not yet, at least. Not as long as big oaks produce little acorns.

Index